Too Many Tears

FIONA DOYLE

PENGUIN BOOKS

PENGUIN BOOKS

Published by the Penguin Group
Penguin Books Ltd, 80 Strand, London WC2R ORL, England
Penguin Group (USA) Inc., 375 Hudson Street, New York, New York 10014, USA
Penguin Group (Canada), 90 Eglinton Avenue East, Suite 700, Toronto, Ontario, Canada M4P 2Y3
(a division of Pearson Penguin Canada Inc.)
Penguin Ireland, 25 St Stephen's Green, Dublin 2, Ireland
(a division of Penguin Books Ltd)
Penguin Group (Australia), 707 Collins Street, Melbourne, Victoria 3008, Australia
(a division of Pearson Australia Group Pty Ltd)
Penguin Books India Pvt Ltd, 11 Community Centre,
Panchsheel Park, New Delhi – 110 017, India
Penguin Group (NZ), 67 Apollo Drive, Rosedale, Auckland 0632, New Zealand
(a division of Pearson New Zealand Ltd)
Penguin Books (South Africa) (Pty) Ltd, Block D, Rosebank Office Park, 181 Jan Smuts
Avenue, Parktown North, Gauteng 2193, South Africa

Penguin Books Ltd, Registered Offices: 80 Strand, London WC2R ORL, England

www.penguin.com

First published by Penguin Ireland 2013
Published in Penguin Books 2014
001

Copyright © Fiona Doyle, 2014

Typeset by Palimpsest Book Production Ltd, Falkirk, Stirlingshire
Printed in Great Britain by Clays Ltd, St Ives plc

ISBN: 978–1–844–88323–3

www.greenpenguin.co.uk

MIX
Paper from
responsible sources
FSC C018179

Penguin Books is committed to a sustainable
future for our business, our readers and our planet.
This book is made from Forest Stewardship
Council™ certified paper.

This book is dedicated to my wonderful husband,
Jim, and my children.

I also dedicate it to all victims of rape and sexual abuse,
male and female. Don't let your abuse define you.
It's a part of you, not *all* of you. Talking is power.
Speak out and take your power back.

My wish is that this book will give someone else
the strength to speak out.

1. Daddy's Favourite

I'm holding the cup by the handle, walking slowly, carefully, step by step up the stairs, trying not to spill the hot coffee. If I do I'll be in trouble with my mammy. She told me to carry it up to my daddy, who is in bed. I see him sitting up in bed when I get to the door of their room. He's looking at something. 'Nearly there,' I think, as I concentrate hard on getting the cup of coffee over to him without it sloshing out. I leave it down on the bedside locker. Lean in to see what he's looking at. They're playing cards but different to the ones I play Snap with when I play cards with my sisters and brothers. These ones have pictures of men and women on them. They have no clothes on. They're doing things I don't understand. Bending over one another. My daddy picks one up and shows it to me. 'Do you know what she's doing?' he asks me. 'Yes, Da,' I say. 'She's eating a sausage.' This makes him laugh. I smile. He opens his pyjamas and takes out his willy. I've seen my brother's before, when he was being washed, but my daddy's is very different. Ugly. I don't want to look at it. I go to turn away. 'She was licking that,' he tells me. He orders me to do it to him. I don't want to. I want to go back downstairs now, to the others. He leans over to me and brings my head down into his lap. I'll never forget the smell.

I was about four years old.

I was born in May 1966, the second child in the family. I had an older brother, Austin, and three younger siblings: two sisters, Christine and Laura, and a brother, Richard. Austin was a year older than me, Christine a year younger, Laura was three years younger and Richard five years younger. The house that we lived in during our childhood was in Mackintosh Park in Dun Laoghaire. It was rented from the council. It was an ordinary three-bedroom house, part of a terrace of houses that all looked the same. It was in a big estate. There was a field in front.

My parents were Patrick and Bridget (known as Breda) O'Brien. My mother's maiden name was Burke. She came from Sallynoggin in Dublin. I don't know how or where she and my father met. I don't remember it ever being talked about in our house. She's one of a family of eight and had three brothers and four sisters. One of her brothers is dead. My dad had two brothers and a sister. My father worked for a local building company as a labourer for years. Then he worked for a time for a company installing televisions in the area. He had to give up work when he developed deep-vein thrombosis. After that he stayed home and my mother went out to work. She held a series of jobs over the years, working in factories and as a cleaner.

My early years all blend together but the memory of my First Communion is seared on my mind. Think of a seven-year-old little girl, all excited about her big day – about the dress, about being in the big church with all the other girls, spending the day with her family, being treated. My Communion Day was very different.

My mammy is out at bingo. My daddy has called me out of bed to make him coffee. I take a deep breath and go downstairs. I have just my nightie on. I go to the kitchen and put the kettle on. I stand there waiting on it to boil and my stomach turns. I know what is going to happen. I'm cold. I am making my First Communion tomorrow. I just want to go back to bed.

I carry the coffee into the sitting room. My daddy is sitting on his chair beside a blazing fire. I put the coffee on the mantelpiece and turn to him. Waiting for what he's going to tell me to do. He says to lie on the sofa and lift my nightie up. I have no panties on. We aren't allowed to wear them in bed. My father gets up and moves me into the position he wants me in. He drops his trousers and underpants and gets on top of me. I can hardly breathe with the weight of him. As I turn my head to try to breathe I am right at his armpit. The smell of sweat is awful. He forces his willy into me. I'm so sore and it burns. He pushes it in as far as it'll go. I turn my head to watch the telly to take my mind off it. I put my fingers in my mouth to stop myself from screaming. I can't make noise or I'll be in big trouble.

I have pain down below and in my ribs from his weight on me. Finally he makes a grunting noise and I get all wet down below. He gets off me. He doesn't look at me. He tells me to go to bed. I sit up to move. My legs hurt when I try to move them to close them. It's easier to breathe but I'm dizzy.

My nightie falls back down. I go upstairs to bed, walking slowly, step by step. That bad, dirty feeling is back. I reach my bed. Get under the covers. My sisters are giving out to me because I was let watch the telly. I'm burning down below, so sore that I lie on my side. I go to sleep with my hands down between my legs, trying to stop the pain. I hope he doesn't come into my room again later because I'm too sore.

The next morning I got up. Not happy as I should be. Not excited because the soreness reminded me of the night before. I made breakfast as the others gave me dirty looks. They were still annoyed that I was allowed up late to watch television. I had a bath. It didn't help ease the pain and there was blood when I went to the toilet. I went to my mother to get my dress on. She was angry with me. I didn't know why. She scowled at me and pulled me around as she put my dress and veil on. Her nails scratched me. She was calling me names and I didn't know why. When we got to the church I went to sit in a row of other girls in our white dresses and veils, waiting for Mass to start. We'd learned our prayers off by heart. Everyone was whispering to one another in excitement. My mam and dad were sitting behind me with the other mammies and daddies. The hard seat was hurting me. *The other girls are all smiling. Why doesn't it hurt them when their daddies do it to them?* I made myself smile too.

My memory of the day jumps. I don't remember the full day, only the great sense of sadness I was feeling. We went to Stillorgan to see family friends. The elastic in my crocheted knee stockings was too tight and was digging into me, hurting. It left big red marks around my legs. 'What's with the face?' my mother asked me. I told her my socks were hurting me. I couldn't tell her the truth, that I was hurting down below as well. My mother turned to my father and said, 'An ungrateful cunt, that one.' I said no more about it. I did ask later if we were going to see my Nanny Burke, only to be told, 'No, she doesn't want to see you.' I was confused. Hurt. That's not the feeling I got from my nanny, I know it wasn't. She was kind and nice to me. I didn't get to see her that day.

*

4

I'm standing at the kitchen sink. Panic rises inside me. I fight back tears. I'm going to be late for school again. I'm going to get into trouble. I scrub harder, trying to get this cold, sloppy porridge free off the bottom and sides of the pot. I hate the slimy feel of the stuff. If I don't get it cleaned before I go to school my mammy will kill me. She has a very bad temper and I'm afraid of her.

She works and my dad stays at home. It falls to me to do all the jobs around the house and mind my sisters and brothers. I have to do this every morning. Get the others up, get them their breakfast and get their lunches ready. Then they're gone and I'm left to clean up after them. They get to go to school on time. It's not fair.

I went to a local school, Our Lady of Good Counsel in Johnstown in Killiney, for my primary-school years. So did my sister Laura. Austin went to the boys' school right beside our school. Christine and later Richard went to Benincasa Special School on Mount Merrion Avenue in Blackrock. I hated Our Lady of Good Counsel and was very unhappy there. I always felt like an outsider. I wasn't well dressed. I felt the teachers picked on me because I was quiet and absent a lot. Our book bills were never paid and we never went on school tours because our parents wouldn't give us the money.

Homework was never done either, which got me into so much trouble. I was always busy, doing the ironing or making the dinner, there was never the time for homework because if my mother came in from work and the housework wasn't done she would fly into a rage and I was terrified of her. I was frightened and anxious much of the time, trying to keep on top of things so she wouldn't get mad at me.

My mother is screaming at me. I've forgotten to rinse out my underwear. It's hard to remember it every day. I'm shaking, hearing her footsteps coming down the stairs. I'm in for it now. Every day she checks the laundry basket for three pairs of knickers from us girls. If we forget to rinse them out and put them in the basket God help us. I don't understand her strictness over this when the rest of our clothes are shabby a lot of the time. She sends me upstairs to get her dirty underwear from under her pillow too. I hate having to do that.

I'm in the bathroom, at the sink, washing out Richard's terrycloth nappies by hand. The worst job of all. I hate it, the smell, and how hard it is to get them clean. Why do I get all the horrible jobs? Austin is made to wash up and do some cleaning and now that Christine and Laura are bigger they have to help out but I still have to do the most. If there are any mistakes like dirty dishes in the cupboard me and Austin are woken in the middle of the night and, after a few slaps from my mother, are made to wash everything again. We get sent out to the back garden to get the washing from the line in the pitch dark. I'm afraid of the dark but I'm still made go out.

We often had no dinner or electricity but we had the best of furniture. At one stage we had two cars in the driveway even though my mother couldn't drive. It was all about appearances with my mother. She wanted the neighbours to think we were better off than we were. I don't think anyone was fooled though. We had plenty of unpaid bills.

Many a time we had just roast potatoes with tomato sauce to eat because there wasn't anything else. If it was payday we would get a sausage while my mam and dad had steak. That kind of thing went on a lot: we had margarine, they had butter; porridge for us and cornflakes for them.

When they went out we'd nick a taste of their food. We relied a lot on handouts from the St Vincent de Paul. We'd also be sent, regularly, to my nanny and my aunts and uncles for a loan of money or coal for the fire and sometimes for food.

Having sex with my father had a routine. My mother would go out to bingo with my nanny and we would be sent to bed early. After a while my father would call to me to make him a cup of coffee and bring it in to him in the sitting room. When I did he'd tell me to lie down. I'd try to lie in a position that I could see the television from while he was having sex with me. That way I could watch a programme and try to lose myself in it, blocking out what he was doing. When he was finished with me I would be sent upstairs. The others would be angry with me because I'd been allowed down to watch television.

I used to try to stay awake while waiting for my father to call me. I hated being woken up and having to go downstairs, so it was better to try to stay awake. Some nights I'd sit out on the stairs waiting for him to call me and if he hadn't called me by a certain time I'd call out to him, asking if he'd like his coffee now, so that I would be able to see a programme, like *Charlie's Angels*, that I liked. It was my way of handling what was going on and, I think, of trying to have some small bit of control over it. Other times I couldn't handle it at all.

It's a lovely sunny day. It is summer and it's really warm. We are on the beach in Brittas Bay. We are so happy and excited. We don't get brought anywhere very often. We are playing, all of us children, crouched down near the water, digging holes with shells and stones, when I hear my daddy say he's going for a walk. He tells me to go with him. I look over at my mother. She has a funny expression on her face. A knot comes in my stomach. I don't want to go. Not here, not on this day. I want to stay playing with my brothers and sisters. Austin is throwing water on the girls and they are squealing.

He looks at me in a way that means I must go with him. I get up slowly and walk alongside him, across the beach. He is heading for the sand dunes. When we get there he walks around for a while then sits down. I do the same. He has sex with me. I can hear voices. People talking. They don't seem to be that far away. Why doesn't someone walk over the sand dunes to where we are? Why doesn't someone see us? I want someone to catch us but then I think of the shame of being found out.

I don't recall the first time my mother brought it up about me having sex with my father but she was saying it from as far back as I can remember. I say 'having sex with my father' and not 'my father having sex with me' because that's how she saw it, as something that I was doing. Never mind that I was the child and he was the adult, I was the victim and he was the abuser, I had no choice and he did. My mother would call me a 'whore' and a 'slut', words that I didn't understand. She would say I was ruining her marriage. I was confused, my child's mind not able to make sense of what she was saying. What did she want? She used to wake me and put me in my father's bed and she would stay in mine. She hated me and told me so, often.

My mother used my abuse to get freedom. She would tell my dad she was going somewhere and take the other kids with her, leaving me behind. I hated how that made me feel, abandoned and isolated. One time we were all asked to my cousin's birthday party. We were so excited because we never had parties or presents or even cards on our birthdays and we loved going to our aunt and uncle's house. When we were dressed and ready to go my mother and father started a row and in the end my mother shouted, 'I'll go with the others and leave your tramp behind with you!' They went off without me to the party.

I cried for hours over that. When they came back I heard my mother telling my father that she told my aunt I wasn't brought because I was bold. My aunts and uncles were told that quite often.

I am ten years old now. I'm in school. It is summertime. The sun is coming in through the windows. We are being given a talk. It's about good touches and bad touches and how we should tell somebody if someone touches us in a way that makes us feel uncomfortable. We must tell someone we trust. I realize what my dad is doing to me is wrong. Oh God! I feel my cheeks burn. They are talking about me. I look around to see if anyone is looking at me. They're not, they're all looking up at the woman giving the talk. After that she tells us how to recognize someone who's had that done to them. They are usually quiet, she says, and don't join in with things or mix much with other children. I look around the classroom again and then up at my teacher. 'You're not very bright,' I think, 'if you can't see that in me.'

My father stood up for me when my mother verbally and physically abused me. He'd tell her to stop but that only made it worse. A row would start, shouting and screaming. Their arguments were terrible, often we wouldn't be able to sleep or we'd be woken up and hear the furniture being smashed and my mother getting a beating. Some beatings were so bad my mother had to go to hospital. One time, when I was about twelve, they were fighting and my father called out to me to make him a cup of coffee. I did what I was told and when I carried it in my mother started to call me names. My father took the scalding coffee off me and threw it over my mother. She went for me, saying I'd made it especially for him to throw over her. I didn't. I hated seeing her hurt. Broken fingers, stitches, she had them all. The gardaí were even called a few times and all the neighbours knew.

I'm in the car with my daddy. He's driving around. It's dark outside. I know it's late. I'd been in bed, asleep, when we were woken by him and Mammy fighting. She roared at him to take his slut, by which she meant me, and get out. He came upstairs and got me out of bed, told me to get dressed. I hate it when this happens.

I know what's coming. Driving around for the night, stopping in lay-bys to have sex with me. If he stays away for more than one night I'll go hungry because he never has any money. I'll miss school and be in trouble again.

I went back to Our Lady of Good Counsel after Christmas the year I was twelve to learn that I'd be making my Confirmation in a few weeks' time. It was the first I knew of it because I'd been absent before Christmas. I missed a lot of school over the years, for various different reasons. I would be made to stay home sometimes as punishment. My mother knew I'd get into trouble over missing days. Other times it was to do jobs she wanted done. Making my Confirmation at that time meant Austin and I would be confirmed together. I was delighted and all excited. I couldn't wait to get home to tell my mother the news. I thought she'd be pleased. She was quite the opposite.

She flew into a rage and I got beaten. She went on and on about the expense of having two Confirmations together. As the date neared she went to the St Vincent de Paul, looking for help.

They gave her a voucher to take to a big store in Dublin. She took me with her but didn't let me choose my own outfit, as many of the girls in my class were allowed to do. Instead she picked a suit for me that I thought was far too old-fashioned and dowdy. It was blue and made of a kind of tweed material. I hated it. I dreaded the thought of wearing it when the day came. I had to though; I had no choice.

I felt I stood out from the other girls, who all had fashionable outfits. Other than that, I have no memory of the day. I remember feeling very aggrieved when, in the years that followed, first Christine and then Laura got to choose their own outfits for their Confirmation. I harboured that resentment for a long, long time.

After my Confirmation I was moved to a different school. Laura was too. I wasn't told why we were being moved from Our Lady of Good Counsel in Killiney to the Dominican Convent in Dun Laoghaire. I only had a year to do, repeating sixth class, which I needed to do because

I'd missed so much time. Looking back I think we were moved because my parents were afraid my teachers would see evidence of the physical punishment I was subjected to, or have suspicions about the sexual abuse. I don't know what our first school was told but suddenly we were going to the Dominican.

It was hard, starting over at a new school where I knew no one. There was the problem all over again of missing time and having no money for books and other stuff at the new school. I hated having to explain myself, to be constantly making excuses. I had to wear a school uniform there. It sticks out in my mind because my mother complained about having to buy it. It was a drab brown jumper and skirt with a cream blouse. Laura and I had a school photograph taken while wearing them. It stays in my mind for another reason too. My father abused me many times while I was wearing that uniform.

I didn't have any school friends during my years in Our Lady of Good Counsel. I found it hard to make friends. I was very insecure and self-conscious. I knew instinctively that I was different, set apart somehow from others my age. I did make some friends when I was moved to the Dominican Convent but I was never allowed go to their houses after school and I never wanted to invite them to mine. I didn't have any friends on our road at home either, I never had time to be out among them, I always had housework to do inside and, besides, I wouldn't have been allowed out on our street by my mother and father. They kept very tight control of me, more so than my sisters and brothers. I didn't make friends when I went to secondary school either. I felt I had little in common with the other girls there.

Austin and I got most of the beatings, growing up. We were beaten with everything and anything, whatever was near. A dog lead. A poker. Austin stupidly supplied the poker. When he was in Cabinteely Community School he made it in metalwork class and brought it home as a present. The next time my father needed something to beat us with, he used it. I blamed Austin for bringing it home and we had a big fight. Sometimes the beatings would be for trivial things like forgetting to make them coffee and bringing it up before we left for school. The beatings went on and the abuse went on. It was part of my life.

I'm sitting in the waiting room in St Michael's Hospital in Dun Laoghaire. I am holding a towel to my eye. It hurts but I'm afraid to cry again. I've already been told to shut up. I wonder how Austin is. He wasn't brought to the hospital with us. It started with my mother saying money was missing from her purse. She lined the five of us up. She was screaming at my father that we were getting out of hand, saying he didn't hit us enough. He got one of the metal bits of tube from the Hoover and started lashing out at us.

We huddled in a corner with Austin turning his back, trying to protect us. He got the most lashes. His back was in a state. I got a few lashes on the arms because I'd put them up to protect myself. Then I felt a sting as the edge of the tube caught me on the eye. There was blood everywhere. Here now in the hospital I'm told again to tell them I fell. My wrist hurts too. I hear my name being called. We follow the nurse. My eye is stitched. 'I fell,' I tell them.

Why didn't anyone notice the trouble I was in? Even the

family doctor I was taken to because I kept getting head-aches didn't say anything. I was allowed to go in to him alone when my mother took me to see him. He asked me what was wrong – was I under stress? How was school? All questions I couldn't answer. I was taken to him for another reason one day: I had what felt like lumps in my back passage. I was thirteen years old.

My mother was told I had genital warts. I didn't understand at the time what they were, or how or why I had got them. I was sent to hospital to have them removed by laser. I was kept in hospital for three days. It made me feel really dirty and yet I didn't understand why. It was much later that I learned they are a form of sexually transmitted disease. Why didn't my doctor or the hospital ask questions? How did I get them when I was so young? I figured out that no one was to be trusted and so I didn't trust anyone. I just kept my mouth shut. The sex became no big deal to me, it was just part of my life. I didn't know any different and I could no longer remember a time when it wasn't happening.

I came home after school one day and my mother and father were upstairs arguing. She came thundering down the stairs, saying she was going to ring the gardaí to tell them I was sleeping with my father. I was in the kitchen. The phone was in the hall. I heard her pick it up, heard her press numbers. I was terrified. I stood completely still, in fear and shock. I felt my legs go weak. *What would happen to me when she told them? Would I be taken away? Would I be put in jail?* She put the phone down without talking to anyone and I realized she had only been pretending. I was so relieved.

Not long after – I must have been about fourteen because I recall that I was wearing the distinctive red jumper of the Cabinteely Community School uniform – my mother kicked my father and me out of the house. We went to my aunt and uncle's house in Blackrock. (I discovered later that they weren't really related to us, they were friends of our parents but we knew them as our uncle and aunt.) I was upset because I was on a debating team the next day in school and wanted to be home so I could get to school. I was told to go to bed. A few hours later, my father came in and got into bed with me.

Early the next morning my mother came to the house and burst into the room, shouting, 'I told you you were sleeping with her!' My father shouted at her to get out and she went outside and waited until he got dressed. When they were all in the sitting room they were arguing about him sleeping with me. My 'aunt' and 'uncle' were there. I had got dressed and was outside in the hallway, listening. I was shaking. I was so worried about what was going to happen but my father just kept denying it, saying he was dressed while he was in bed with me. He said that he was just trying to comfort me because I was upset after being called names and being thrown out of the house by my mother.

After a day of my parents fighting I was brought home and my mother chose to believe that my father had his clothes on. My brothers and sisters believed I was getting lots of attention and they resented me for it. I can't really blame them for thinking that. And I was in such trouble with my classmates for letting them down, I was never asked to take part in anything again.

As I got older my father would often take me outside the house to have sex. I think it was because the others were getting older too and there was a chance they'd catch him abusing me in the house. He took me to different places. Once it was the golf course in Foxrock. A few times it was the local cemetery where my grandparents were buried. He would clean and tidy up his parents' grave and headstone first and then, when he was finished, he'd take me into nearby trees to rape me.

2. No Escape

I loved my aunts and uncles; I have a lot of nice memories of them. Some lived near us in Ireland and, as I've said, we would often be sent to them with notes, looking for loans of money and, sometimes, food. We would be given chocolate bars and cakes in their houses, which were such a treat for us. I would think of excuses to stay longer than I should have with them when I was sent. Yet my mother always said they didn't want us. I couldn't understand it at the time; it was so confusing because it was at odds with how nice they were to us and how well they cared for us.

I loved babysitting for one uncle and aunt in particular. Des was my mother's brother. They lived in Sallynoggin at that time, which wasn't far from us. It was great in Des and Alice's house, everyone was happy and there were no arguments. The house felt so calm compared to ours. It was always warm in winter. Alice baked a lot and made lovely dinners. I used to be so happy when my uncle called and took me on his motorbike to babysit. They'd leave out sweets and other goodies for me and their kids while they went out. Sometimes my mother would tell Christine to go instead of me and I hated that, I always wanted to be the one that went, to escape our house for a while.

I think Des knew something of my difficulties at home because the next day, after babysitting, he and Alice would usually let me stay on for a while with them and I would, because I loved being in their house, but I did it in the certain knowledge that I'd be in big trouble with my mother and father when I got home.

My father hated it when I wasn't around him but I didn't care, it was worth it to spend the time at Des and Alice's, watching a normal, happy family. My nanny lived with them and she was so kind to us too. It was so confusing because of my mother continually telling us that we weren't wanted by them.

Things came to a head though after one occasion when I was babysitting for Des and Alice. I was about thirteen. They got back late and I was allowed to stay the night in their house. The next morning Alice was up early, making breakfast for everyone. I wasn't used to that and I sat happily chatting away to her, in my head wishing I could stay for ever. Not for the first time I wished they were my mam and dad. Alice asked if I'd like to stay a few days with them. 'Oh yes,' I said. I couldn't help it. I knew I was supposed to say 'no' and go home. Des or Alice rang my mother to tell her I was staying for a few days. 'I will be killed when I get home,' I thought, but still I wanted to stay. I never wanted to leave.

After a couple of days I began to worry. I knew I had to get home, so I asked if I could walk on back to our house. It wasn't that far. The Lourdes Hospital was between the estate I lived in and Sallynoggin Park, but if I cut through the hospital grounds it would be shorter, so I set out for home. I hated that walk and had to force myself on.

As soon as I got in the door I knew something was wrong.

My mother was in the kitchen. There were broken cups and plates all over the place. My mother was at the sink, holding her hand under the cold water. I saw that she had a huge blister on her hand. The whole back of her hand and fingers were swollen and bright red. It's the first time I ever remember feeling sorry for her.

'What happened?' I asked, shocked at the sight. 'Are you OK?'

She looked at me with hate. 'This is your fault, you tramp, you little whore, why did you stay over there, you knew he would go mad.'

She kept calling me names. I started to cry. 'I'm sorry,' I sobbed. I didn't want her hurt, really I didn't. She called me more names and began throwing stuff at me. I ran out of the kitchen and upstairs to my bed. I really didn't want to see my mammy hurt. I didn't plan it, like she said. I felt so bad. I tried to make it up to her by doing as much cleaning as I could. I cleared up all of the broken stuff and I made the dinner. I could see she was in pain.

My brothers and sisters were mad with me too; they told me there'd been a big fight between our parents because I had stayed at Des and Alice's house. My mother had shouted at my father, asking him if he missed 'his tramp', and he flew into a rage and poured the scalding water over her hand. I cried and told myself I wouldn't stay away again. Every time I tried to help, my mother would take swipes at me and call me names. My father also hit me when he saw me and told me, 'Don't you ever stay out of this house again without asking.' I realized that I couldn't go anywhere.

I hated the way my mother treated me but I really didn't

want to see her hurt. My father raped me that night. I can't remember where my mother was. I knew then that what she'd said was right; that was the reason for him scalding my mother – he was angry because he needed his 'whore', as she put it.

Nanny Burke used to come to our house to make sure my mother was OK. She was always telling my mother not to be so nasty to me but my mam kept telling her how badly behaved I was. Yet Nanny was never angry with me. I couldn't understand it. If Nanny didn't want us and was told I was so bold why was she always so nice and kind? Sometimes we would be stopped from seeing my nanny for months and we never knew why.

Nanny is looking lovely in her green suit. I love seeing her in that. She is such a lady. She's come to visit on a bad day though. My mammy and daddy are in the middle of a big row. There's a lot of shouting. I don't want my nanny seeing them like that. I don't want her to be upset. She goes into the sitting room with them. After a while I hear my name being called. I go in and my daddy says, 'Go on, tell her.' My nanny says to my mother not to. She says it in a sad kind of way. I look at my nanny. She looks like she is going to cry. I want to go over to her but I stand where I am, inside the door, looking down at the floor. My father looks at my mother and says to her again, 'She's here now. Go on, tell her.'

My mammy turns to me. 'Fiona, I hate the breath you draw and the ground you walk on,' she says. I dig my nails into my hand. I swallow hard. I don't say anything. My nanny gets up from the chair and rushes out past me and down the hall towards the front door. I can hear her crying.

That was one of the last times I saw my nanny before she had her stroke. It happened a couple of days later. Even then my mother didn't show any emotion. She was such a cold person. After the stroke my nanny had to go into a nursing home. It was in Dun Laoghaire. I used to sneak down to visit her there. After she was in the nursing home for about a year she passed away.

We're on a holiday with my aunt in Wembley in London again. She is my dad's sister. It is Christmas time. I am fourteen years old. This is the second time we've come to England on our holidays. The first time, a year ago, also to this same aunt, we were taken to Bognor Regis for the day. It's a town by the seaside about two hours from Aunt Phyllis's. It was good fun but I remember it too because Dad got so angry with me. We were at the beach and I was out in the water, floating around in a rubber ring. My cousin's husband was with us. He was about twenty-five. Dad accused me of flirting with him.

As a thirteen-year-old kid I barely knew what 'flirting' was and I certainly wouldn't have had the confidence to flirt with anyone. But my father didn't see it that way. It was more of his extreme possessiveness and jealousy over me. I was in my teens now, no longer a child, and I think he feared losing control over me.

This time I've been asked to stay in my cousin's house. She is expecting a baby and my aunt says I can help her. I love being here. I'm away from my mother and father. My daddy doesn't like it though. He wants me staying at my aunt's where the rest of them are. I say no. I want to stay here. My daddy is narky with me because of it. I just try to stay out of his way. Today I was going to the shop on a message for my cousin and my daddy followed me. I stayed on the far side of the road but when we got back to my aunt's he snapped and started to beat me really badly, shouting at me that I had ignored him.

When my aunt tried to stop him and asked him why he was hitting me, he just said again that I was ignoring him. I was beaten black and blue in my aunt's hall and I couldn't say anything. My father and mother told her I was uncontrollable. I couldn't tell her why he was really beating me. They all think now that I'm badly behaved. No one will believe me.

I can't recall if my dad had sex with me on that holiday. I switched off. I would go into a world of my own. I felt so alone during those years.

I don't remember much about Christmas in our house, not most of them anyway. But there was one that sticks out. I had just turned fifteen. I had seen a watch in a local jewellers; it was gold with love hearts engraved all around it. I really wanted that watch and kept going on about it.

I was, at this stage, allowed to go to the kids' roller disco in Dun Laoghaire sometimes on a Sunday afternoon. One Sunday just before Christmas a fella there asked me to dance. I couldn't believe it. Not one fella had ever shown an interest in me before. He asked me to meet him the next Sunday, which would have been straight after Christmas. God, I was happy! I was so excited. I felt attractive. I couldn't wait for next Sunday to come.

I'm lying in bed. I've stopped crying. My body is sore, my arms aching from where my father hit them as I tried to protect myself from the beating. He was in a rage, beating me like he was never going to stop. I'd been so looking forward to going to the roller disco today. On Christmas Day I'd got the watch I wanted. I couldn't believe it. It was beautiful. I would wear it to the roller disco. My father though had decided I wasn't going. He had found out why I wanted to go.

My mother had taken me aside and told me not to mind him, to go ahead to the disco, so in the middle of the morning I snuck out and went up the road to get the bus. The roller disco started in the afternoon. I wanted to get there early.

I was standing waiting for the bus, looking down at my watch, twisting my hand this way and that, admiring it, when my father pulled up in the car and screamed at me to get in. As soon as I was in the car he started to punch me in the face and call me names. When I got home he started in on me again. He pulled the watch off my wrist and flung it on the floor. When he was finished I was told to go to bed and stay there.

My mother hasn't even come to see if I'm all right and yet she had told me to go. Lying here now in the dark, sore from the beating and with a headache from crying, I'm thinking that she must have told him after I left where I was going. I turn my face to the wall, pull the bedcovers up over my head. I just can't take any more. My life is hell.

A little while later I got up and went into my parents' bedroom. In the bedside locker were a lot of tablets belonging to my mother. I swallowed them all. I really wanted it all to end. A bit later my brother Austin came upstairs to check on me. We'd always been there for one another. He'd heard about the beating and came up to see how I was. I told him what I had done. He ran out of the room, went downstairs and told my mother. She wanted to ring an ambulance but my father wouldn't let her so she made me drink strong black coffee and I was terribly sick.

Later on that night I was sent to babysit for their friends.

As for the watch, well that was gone, and so was the guy. I never got to see him again. I didn't try going out after that.

Not for the first time Austin had tried to help me, but he had a job looking after himself. He stayed out of the house as much as possible. He had made friends with some men down at the docks in Dun Laoghaire and spent a lot of time down there with them. Mam and Dad didn't seem to care where he was. He would stay out for two or three days in a row. One day he came home for clean clothes and my mother started to fight with him and hit him because he was dirty and she told him to get out and stay out. He left and that night I could see him sleeping in the field across from our house. It broke my heart. I was so worried about him, it was cold and he must have been freezing.

When my mother left for work the next morning and my father was still in bed I let Austin into the house. He collected up his stuff, packed it, and said he was leaving and he wouldn't be back. He had been my ally. Now I really was all alone.

Austin has been gone a couple of weeks. I really miss him. I decided to run away myself and I thought about it for a few days. But here I am back in my own bed – I can't even run away properly. I'm a disaster.

Earlier tonight, at about ten o'clock, I climbed out the bedroom window and ran up the road to the bus stop. I only had 20p but I decided to take the bus as far as the 20p would get me. I planned in my head to go to Dublin, I don't know why. I didn't have any kind of plan after that. I sort of thought that when I got to Dublin someone would discover me and I'd be taken to where there'd be people in charge who could arrange for me to live somewhere else and not have to go back home again.

The bus only took me as far as Donnybrook and then I had to get off. It was late and very dark. I came across a field and went in, lay down and tried to sleep but I couldn't. I was cold and afraid of the dark. I didn't know what to do but I knew I couldn't stay there. I got up again, made my way out of the field and started to walk back. I walked as far as Blackrock and was so scared of the night by then that I went to my mam and dad's friends; they put me in their car and took me home.

I was expecting a beating but my parents just sent me to bed because their friends were still downstairs with them, talking. 'I'm in for it in the morning,' I think.

I had been away four hours. They'd found out I was gone but they hadn't reported me missing.

The arguments between my mam and dad got worse. Then one day, when I was fifteen, my mother told me that our house was up for sale and we were moving to England. I think she and my father believed a fresh start was what they needed to help them get along better. Or maybe, given the hand-to-mouth existence we lived, they were keeping one step ahead of people we owed money to. I'm not sure. In any case it was decided.

Austin by now was already living in England with an aunt and uncle, another of my mother's brothers. My mother told me she was going ahead with the three younger kids and I was staying behind with my father while he waited for the house to sell. She told me he wouldn't have stayed without me. I was devastated. I don't understand why I felt so hurt. I knew my mother didn't want me. I can't explain how confused I felt; I wanted to go with my mother, I really did, even though I knew she didn't want me.

The commotion has been going on since the early hours. My mother, not usually awake early, has been up for a couple of hours. She's stamping up and down the stairs, shouting at my sisters and brother to get up, get moving. Christine and Laura get up straight away and get dressed, excited that this is the day they're going on the ferry. They don't say goodbye to me, just leave the room.

My mother is shouting instructions at my father now. I'm lying in bed, listening to it all going on. I don't want to get up. Can't bear to see them with all their bags packed, getting ready to leave. The knot in my stomach is back. I've been crying since I woke up. I'm waiting to hear my mother's feet on the stairs, expecting her to come into my room and say something before she goes.

I hear more commotion then the sound of the front door slamming. They're gone. My mother hasn't even come to say goodbye. I am sobbing now, scarcely able to believe it, that they really have gone and left me. I am fifteen years old. I've been left at home for my father to rape whenever he wants.

I wasn't in my own bed after that. I was moved into my father's room and there I stayed for a few months. I spent the days packing what was left behind, cleaning the house so it would look nice when buyers came to view it, and sleeping with my father every night.

I really started to resent my mother. Why did she leave me behind? I knew the answer. She had got her freedom. She would ring and talk to my dad and never ask about me. The other kids had started school over there and were getting on well, but me, I was out of school now. I think the school assumed I had gone to England with the others. The hurt of being left behind just wouldn't go away. I couldn't shake it. I was so unhappy.

My dad started to notice. One night I was in bed and I was crying. He kept asking me what was wrong. He started to cry also, saying that he shouldn't be sleeping with me and that he was going to stop. He got a knife and held it to his wrist and said he was going to kill himself. I got scared and begged him not to do it but he just kept crying and saying how sorry he was and that he should stop and this was the only way. I didn't know what to do. I begged him not to kill himself and in the end I said that what he was doing was OK. Yes, that's right; I said it was OK. OK for him to sleep with me. Can you believe it? So he got into bed and had sex with me. I lay there awake after he'd finished, thinking: there is no getting out.

It wasn't the only time he used the threat of suicide to coerce me into having sex with him. He used every means possible to manipulate me.

I am sick with worry. My period hasn't come. Suppose I'm pregnant? Oh God, please God no. Please, please God no. After a few weeks I tell my dad. I am frantic with worry. I can't eat, I can't sleep. I can't concentrate on anything. He doesn't seem too concerned. Tells me he's decided, if I am pregnant, that he will tell people that I snuck out one night to be with a fella. Does he not understand that it's not just about not wanting people to know he'd be the father? That I don't want a baby at fifteen? That there is also the fear of how my mother will react? I am so worried and stressed.

What will I do? I can't have a baby. But it hasn't made him stop or take precautions while having sex with me. My Aunt Pearl, my mother's sister, is trying to look after me. She keeps telling my dad to bring me over to her house in Ballybrack for dinner. I think she is surprised I've been left behind and she keeps asking what's up with me. I can't tell her my period hasn't come. We went over there the other night and my father started to tell her this big long story about me sneaking out at night and that he had found out I'd been with a fella. When my aunt asked me about it I had to say I did. I could tell she was angry with me. All my aunts and uncles are being told how uncontrollable I am and while all this is going on I'm still worried sick about being pregnant.

After a few weeks my period came. I think it was delayed by sheer worry and stress. That was the worst time.

3. Finally Shouting 'Stop'

The house still wasn't sold. My dad decided to go and visit my mother in England. I can't remember if I was supposed to go but in the end I was left behind anyway. My Aunt Pearl in Ballybrack said I could stay with them, she had just had a new baby and I was asked to be godmother. I was so pleased and proud. I had a good time with them and wished I could stay there for ever. I kept daydreaming about that happening, wishing my mam and dad would decide they didn't want me over there with them, and letting me stay with my aunt and uncle for good. But of course it didn't happen. My dad came back. I don't know how long it went on, me being left behind in Ireland before the house was sold. I was finally taken to England. I was sixteen by then.

We are all staying in our uncle and aunt's house in Derby. Tom is one of my mother's brothers. It's very cramped with us all here. A few weeks have passed. I wonder when we'll be getting a house of our own. My mother and father have gone back to Ireland to sign papers to fix up the sale of the house in Dun Laoghaire. I've been left to look after the younger ones. I don't mind. I love the peace in my head when our parents are not around. They've been gone for about three weeks now so I'm guessing they'll be back soon. I get stressed when I think of them coming back.

I'm starting to enjoy my freedom for the first time. I'm making friends and having fun. I joined the local swimming pool. It's just next door to the house. Even though I'm minding my sisters and little brother I'm enjoying myself.

I was so disappointed when they arrived back. I was relieved at least to be staying in my cousin's bedroom as it meant my dad wasn't able to get at me. I knew deep down though that trouble would start sooner or later and sure enough it did. My parents started to argue as badly as ever. I would lie in bed and listen to them. So would the rest of the house. My uncle and aunt were getting upset with it all. My mam and dad were sleeping in the sitting room so everyone in the house could hear them when they fought. The language and the name-calling were terrible and it went on night after night. I would shut it out by drifting off into a world of my own.

It wasn't long before my dad noticed I was avoiding him and he started going on to my mother about me swimming and being out with my friend. They began grounding me for no reason. My aunt and uncle saw what was going on and kept asking why I wasn't allowed out and was being grounded. They could see I wasn't badly behaved. My father soon got a chance to get me on my own. I was upstairs and everyone else was downstairs when he called me into the bedroom and asked me out straight why I was avoiding him.

I got brave and told him I didn't want him to touch me again and he asked why. He said it wasn't dirty. I asked him what he meant. I could see he was getting angry.

'You shouldn't be doing it, it is dirty,' I said.

'Are you saying I'm a dirty old man?' he asked.

'Yes,' I said, and I ran out of the room.

I knew then that there'd be trouble and I stayed out of his way. It was a couple of weeks before he exploded. I didn't see it coming.

It started this afternoon with my father shouting at us, 'You three girls, get out to the car. I want to speak to you.' We go out and get into the back of the car. I get in the middle, between Laura and Christine. A stupid move. I should have been more careful. He is going on about us getting out of hand. He says I'm going swimming to meet lads, that I'm turning into a right tramp. I start to argue with him but he shouts at me and says he's bringing me to London. He starts the car. He leans around and punches me a couple of times in the stomach. I am winded, the breath whooshed out of me. I can't breathe properly. I'm panicking. Christine and Laura are crying. I get my breath back and start to scream. I don't want to be taken away to London.

My mother comes out and hears me screaming. He's gunning the engine now so she runs and jumps into the front of the car as he's driving off. My mother is shouting at him to stop. She's asking him what's wrong, what's happened. He tells her I'm getting out of hand and turning into a tramp. I'm crying. She tells him to stop the car and let her and the girls out. He stops the car and my mother gets out of the front. As Christine and Laura go to get out of the back I try getting out with them, pushing Laura ahead of me so I can make it. He goes mad, driving off with us still in the back, leaving my mother behind. We're all howling now.

I keep saying 'I'm sorry.' He begins to calm down again. He turns the car around and goes back for my mother. She gets in the car and we drive back towards my uncle's house. On the way my mother asks me what it was I said to upset my dad. He tells her I called him a dirty old man. They start arguing again. He's calling me awful names. He tells her that unless I take back what I said he'll ram the car into a

wall. She turns around and shouts to me, 'Take it back!' I say 'no'
because in my mind they are trying to get me to agree to say that having
sex with him is OK. He gets angry again and starts to drive the car at
a wall. Christine and Laura are screaming and my mother is roaring
at me to take it back. My dad is shouting, 'I'm going to ram the car!'

All I can see is the wall coming towards us. 'OK, OK, I'm sorry, I
take it back,' I hear myself say. I am shaking. He has slowed to a
stop. Christine and Laura are looking at me as if they hate me. He
turns the car around and drives back to the house.

My uncle and aunt were frantic, they had heard us screaming before the car drove off and had rung the police. When
my dad saw the police arrive at their house he grabbed a
knife and ran into the bathroom. I don't know what they
were told but the police threatened to take Christine, Laura
and Richard. They couldn't take me. I was told I was too
old. The only reason the police agreed to leave was on condition that my dad left the house and went to stay in a hotel.
He did but kept ringing the house, crying all the time, and
my mother would put me on the phone because she said
what had happened was all my fault.

My uncle and aunt were at their wits' end at this stage,
they couldn't cope with it all, the rows, the shouting, and
now this. My father came back to the house a week later but
the arguments never stopped and finally my uncle and aunt
asked them to leave.

We were on the move again. This time we all went to Luton
to my dad's brother's house. My mother and father told
them a pack of lies, saying they didn't know why we had
been thrown out. They never said anything about the inci-

dent with the car and the police being involved. We stayed in Luton for a while and still I never let him get to me. I had decided 'no more'. I got to see Austin again. He was in a hostel and was happy and I was happy for him. After a while the rest of us moved out of Luton and back to Derby, where my mam and dad bought a house.

I turned seventeen and I had a place in college, the Wilmorton College of Further Education in Derby, to do a City & Guilds course in hotel management. I enjoyed going there. My father didn't like me going but I kept at it and was doing well. His violence continued. One night during a row at home he was beating my mother at the foot of the stairs. I came out to the landing to see Austin standing there. I shouted at him to do something but he didn't move. It was like he was frozen.

I ran down and screamed at my father to take his hands off her. Poor Austin, he was only just back for the weekend. I felt so bad. My dad went for me and hit me. I legged it back to the room I shared with my sisters. He shouted at me that I was out of control and he was locking me up for my own good. He locked the bedroom door. He unlocked it to let my sisters out to go to school the next morning but he wouldn't let me go to college. My mother unlocked the door and told me to go while he wasn't looking.

I'm in the social services office in Derby. After I left the house I walked miles to get here. I had to ask for directions to their office. I'm with a social worker here now. I am nervous and anxious but still angry at being locked in my room. I tell the social worker my father locked me up and that I got out. She's asking me if there's anything going on with my father. Anything 'inappropriate'. I hear myself saying no. I don't know why. She tells me she will visit our house and talk to my parents. My heart sinks. Oh God. They'll kill me for bringing social services down on them. I think to myself that I've just made things a hundred times worse by coming here. I leave to walk back home. What a mess.

My mother and father lied when the social workers called to the house, telling them I was running riot and was uncontrollable. The social workers must have believed them because they never came back to me to ask me anything else. I felt so betrayed. I know I didn't tell them the whole truth that day but why didn't they push or ask to see me again? Surely they were trained for that sort of thing, to tease out information from children and teenagers, especially those obviously in distress? It was so frustrating. My father then told me that he wouldn't touch me again. He had obviously gotten a fright by me going to social services. I didn't believe him.

College was my lifeline, and swimming. My course was going well. So well that the college asked me to enrol in another course when that one finished. It would be a two-year course in craft, cookery and bakery. I was one of only three in my class to be offered a place on the course. I think staff at the college saw the potential in me. I was thrilled, it was the first time anyone had shown an interest in me and believed I was good at something. I did the entrance exam and passed and all was going well until I was sent to see the college guidance counsellor to tell me what was involved. In the course of that discussion the subject of fees arose. It turned out that because we hadn't been in the country for two years the government wouldn't pay my fees. I needed £2,000. It was a bitter disappointment. I hadn't told my mother and father about doing this further course; I wanted to see if I got through first. I didn't even bother asking them for the money for fees when I found out we'd have to pay. There was simply no point. I felt a real chance was passing me by. It was hard but I kept my head down and just kept going.

I was on work experience from my hotel management course when I met Joe.[1] I was working at Derby Locomotive Works. As part of my job I had to take the tea trolley around the works each morning. When I was finished with my rounds I was allowed to stay and have a cup of tea with the workers.

After chatting to me one day Joe asked me out and I went. I didn't tell anyone in case I was stopped. He was nine years older than me. He had been married but was separated when I met him. I was impressed that he had a job and his own flat. He seemed so grown up to me and in control of his life. I was so naive and insecure by comparison. I started to see him regularly. We would meet at the swimming pool because it was the only place I was allowed to go. I was flattered by the fact that he showed an interest in me, that he seemed to care for me. For the first time in my life, someone actually cared about me.

When it came to sex I told him he was my first and I didn't tell him about the abuse by my father. I managed to keep the fact that I was seeing him a secret from my family for a while. I even went to the doctor for the pill, though I was scared my mother would find them as she went through my stuff quite often.

After about three months they guessed about Joe and the

---

1 Not his real name.

hassle started again. One night I wanted to go out and my mother wouldn't let me, she told me I had ironing to do. There was a big row and I was called the usual names. I decided I'd had enough. I would leave home. I packed my bags the next day, waited until they were asleep that night, and left.

I went to stay with Joe at his flat; he said it was OK. They thought I'd gone to college that day. In the weeks that followed I stayed away from college in case they'd be waiting for me outside when they discovered I wasn't coming home.

I hid in Joe's flat, afraid to go out or answer the door in case it would be the police. They realized soon enough I'd gone to live with Joe. Austin confirmed it for them.

While all this was going on I heard that a relative had told my parents that Austin had interfered with a young child. I didn't pay much attention to it at the time. I had enough problems of my own. I was pregnant.

Joe is over the moon about the baby. I was shocked at first, but am really happy now that it has sunk in. I went with Joe to tell my mother and father. My dad went mad and attacked Joe in the garden. He had him by the neck. My uncle pulled my dad off Joe.

Things have changed since though, my mam and dad have started to behave differently towards me, keeping in touch to see how I am.

Joe and I have got our own place from the council and moved in. It's a maisonette. I love having a place of our own. My own home. Things are OK apart from the fact that he has to go to court; he was in trouble before he met me, he'd stolen cars and the case is still going on.

What happened to me at that time I don't really understand but it was like it was all gone from my head, the abuse, like it never happened. How could I forget? I don't honestly know, but thoughts of it didn't come into my mind any more. Maybe it was because I was living a more normal life with less worry, tension and stress than I had ever known. It felt good.

I enjoyed, in those months, putting our home together, buying things for it. It was easy to keep clean and tidy. After all, I'd done all the housework and chores since I was a child in the family home as well as looking after my younger sisters and brother. It was a doddle by comparison. Apart from being anaemic I was in good health and loved being pregnant. A baby of my own to love. I couldn't wait for it to be born. Boy or girl, I didn't mind.

I was a week overdue. I was admitted to the Royal Derby Hospital and induced on 8 March 1985, two months away from my nineteenth birthday. I began having contractions and was in labour all day. I was given an epidural and then a second one. Around ten o'clock that night I was taken down to the delivery ward. There were concerns because the baby was in an awkward position and also because of my anaemia. I was frightened and in a lot of pain. They performed an episiotomy on me and then used suction. Finally, when I didn't think I could endure the pain a minute longer, my baby was born. A little girl. I had a daughter. She was taken from me straight away. I wanted to see her and kept asking them to bring her to me. I was stitched up and a while later they brought her back to me.

She was wrapped up tightly in a blanket; all I could see was her face. I wanted to hold her but the nurse said 'no', explaining gently to me that my baby's head was badly swollen from the vacuum. The nurse moved the blanket to show me. My daughter had a big lump on her head and a laceration. Poor little mite. I was assured she would be all right, that her head was soft and that it would return to its normal size within a few days.

4. A Different Kind of Heartache

I was overwhelmed with feelings of love and joy. I'd never before felt anything like it. My mother, father and Austin were waiting outside. Medical staff called my mother in. It was she who suggested the name Kelly. I said yes, I liked it. The nurses kept going on about how beautiful she was. Then, while my mother was standing beside my bed, they unwrapped the baby to show me that one of her little hands had no fingers on it. That arm was smaller than the other as well. I was shocked. My mind was in turmoil. 'You couldn't even have a baby properly,' I was thinking to myself. What a failure I was. Tears welled up. That's why my mother was called in, I realized, so she would be there when they broke the news to me. My mother almost seemed to be being kind to me but I didn't care. All I kept thinking was 'I can't do anything right.' I said it to my mother.

I was wheeled out of the labour ward with my baby daughter. It was after midnight. I saw Austin. He was crying. I cried harder when I saw him. After they all left and I was on the ward with Kelly beside me in a cot, I lay awake looking at her. She was so beautiful. She just lay there looking up at me. I made so many promises to her that night, about all the love I'd give her, the protection I'd make sure she had, always; the chances she'd have in life. Little did I know that night just how hard it would be to try to keep my word to her.

My mother and father and brothers and sisters came to visit the next day with presents for Kelly. It was the first time my mother ever showed real kindness to me.

I was kept in hospital for ten days. Because I had lost so much blood, I needed a transfusion. They kept me in bed with the curtains closed around me. I felt though that it was because they didn't want me to see the other babies in case I rejected Kelly because of her head and her hand. As if I would. I was proud of my daughter. I wanted the world to see her.

When I got home with Kelly I was so happy. I loved my baby girl and she needed me. Someone really needed me. I was doing well with her, coping with the routine of feeding, bathing and changing her. Joe helped me with night feeds and other jobs as well. The swelling on Kelly's head was going down. From the start she sucked her thumb on the little hand that had no fingers. It just melted my heart watching her do that.

I was a bit tired because of the anaemia and I had to have iron injections. I was carrying her down the stairs in the flat a few days after we got home when I got so weak and dizzy that I fell down the stairs. I protected her though, clutching her to my chest, and didn't let her get hurt. I was hurt and frightened by the fall but relieved that she hadn't got injured. She was all that mattered now.

When Kelly was just a couple of weeks old I went into town one day to get her birth registered. While there I decided to have her photo taken by a professional photographer. They were amazed in the shop at how well she could hold her head up while being photographed, and she only a couple of weeks old. I was so proud. I gave the biggest of the photographs to my mother. She had that framed photo on top of her television for years. I kept the smaller ones for myself.

Joe was due in court a few weeks later. When the day came he kissed me goodbye while I was feeding Kelly and said he would see us later. A neighbour and friend went with him. Later on that day as I prepared dinner the friend called to say Joe had got six months' imprisonment. It came as such a shock. I wasn't expecting that. I felt panicked. How would I cope?

My mother and father came and got me and took me to their house overnight. They had lost the house they bought and had been given a council house instead. I spent the next few days crying and worrying about Joe. I returned to our flat and was staying on my own. My mother and father tried to help. They let my sister Christine come to stay with me to keep me company and help me. I was glad to have her.

My parents started talking about moving back to Ireland and made calls about a house to rent in Blackrock. Before I knew it they had a date to move in. Just before they left they came to see me and asked me if they could take Kelly with them so that I could get a job and sort myself out until Joe came out of jail. They would let Christine stay and move in with me. After thinking long and hard I said yes, they could. It sounded reasonable. 'It's only for a short while,' I was thinking. It would allow me to get a job and get back on my feet financially. I let them take her. She was only about three months old. I know that decision might seem strange, to say the least; I was to learn later through counselling why I made certain decisions in my life and behaved in certain ways. Because of having grown up in an abusive situation, I sometimes did things that were not in my best interests, particularly when it came to my parents. Someone with abusive parents will – even when grown up – still sometimes try to win their approval. My parents made me feel that letting them take care of Kelly was the sensible thing for me to do in my circumstances. This was without doubt the biggest mistake of my life.

It is the night before my mam and dad leave for Ireland with Kelly. I'm lying on the bed with her. She's dressed in a pink Babygro. She is looking up at me, smiling, her little legs moving about. Even at this age she is active. I scoop her up and cuddle her. Kiss her head and face. I love her so much. I've never known a love like it. I lay her back down on the bed, arrange her teddy bears beside her and take photos. 'I need these, Kelly, so that I can see you when you're gone,' I tell her.

I plan to stay up all night with her. 'I'm going to miss you so much,' I say, looking down at her. 'But it's only for a little while. I'm going to get a job, get sorted, and you'll soon be back with your mammy.' I take loads of photos. I wish morning will never come.

I got myself a job in a Chinese restaurant, so did Christine and we kept in touch with Austin. He'd met a girl and was living in a council house. I went to visit Joe a good few times in prison and saved hard to buy things for Kelly and him.

Kelly was gone about three months and I was fretting so much for her that I decided to go over to Blackrock to see her. Oh my God, to hold her again was so good, and she had grown so much. I think my mother could see how much I'd missed her. We talked and my parents said I could bring her back to England. I was so happy. I returned to Derby with my precious daughter.

A few weeks later Joe was released from prison and came home at long last. But he had changed. He was angry a lot of the time, picking rows with me. Nothing I did was right. A few weeks after he got out we were having an argument. It was evening time. I was sitting on the bed cuddling Kelly and Joe pulled her out of my arms and threw her onto the bed. He locked all the doors, ripped my clothes off and put a knife to my neck. He kept it there all night. I was crying my eyes out. Things were falling apart. My biggest worry though was that he could have hurt our daughter.

I got in touch with my mother and told her what had happened. I suppose I was just looking for a sympathetic ear, really. Strange, I know, considering that I'd always felt she didn't love me or want me. Three days later she arrived at my door. She said it would be best to take Kelly back to Ireland as it wasn't right for her to be there with all the trouble going on. I agreed to let her go. I wanted her away from Joe. I convinced myself Kelly was better off going. Joe didn't seem to have a problem with her being taken away by my mother and father. For the second time I said good-bye to my infant daughter as she was taken back to Ireland. It never occurred to me, even for a moment, that I might lose her. That I might not get her back.

I tried to carry on. I got another job. Joe and I had drifted apart. He started hanging around with a gang stealing cars and other stuff. Austin was one of the gang. They would come to my home and leave a mess for me to clean. Joe would also keep stolen stuff in the flat, which I hated. I couldn't get him out of the place; his name was on the tenancy agreement too. I was working in a roller disco at the time.

Christmas was coming. I was saving to go to Ireland to spend Kelly's first Christmas with her. Joe was planning on doing his own thing. We had a big row, which ended up with him beating me up pretty badly. After that he moved into Kelly's room.

I was full of resentment towards Joe. I blamed him for me not being able to have my daughter with me. I fretted so much about her. But I was going to see her for Christmas at least. Austin and his girlfriend were going home too; I was travelling with them.

I arrived back in Ireland. My parents had moved again, this time settling in a local authority house in Oldcourt in Bray, Co. Wicklow. I got there during Christmas week. Kelly was great. She had grown so much and was really healthy. I was so happy. It was so good to see her but as I cuddled her she made strange with me, didn't want me. She didn't know me, she wanted my mam and dad. God, it really hurt. I could see though that they were good to her, she had everything she needed. They seemed to be loving her more than I was ever loved. Then they dropped the bombshell: they were adopting her.

We were sitting in the kitchen when they told me. They didn't ask, just said they were adopting her. My mother came out with it, just like that. As matter-of-fact as you like. They had started the proceedings. I could feel myself go ice cold. I looked at her. Said nothing. I was in complete shock. She went on about how it would be for the best. The rest of what they said went over my head. All I could think of was that Kelly was being taken away from me.

I'm in bed now, in their house. Kelly is with them, in their room. I am upset, tossing and turning. What can I offer my baby, with the crap life I have in England? Wouldn't she be better off with them? Could I manage if I were to take her back with me and leave Joe? Would I be able to work and have her with me? I want what's best for her but the thought of not having her with me breaks my heart. I lie awake all night thinking about it.

It never entered my head, the kind of life I'd had growing up and the fact that I'd be leaving my child to be reared by a paedophile. It was as though I had erased it all from my mind. I was in shock and couldn't think straight. At the same time Austin and his girlfriend announced that they were expecting a baby. They were really happy about it. It made me feel even worse. They'd have a baby while mine was being taken away from me. I hadn't even had a period since my beating from Joe – the doctor said it could be stress – so maybe Kelly would be my only baby. Christmas was hell.

In the end I didn't have the heart to pull Kelly away from them. I could see how happy and well treated she was. Instead I went back to England early. I was so depressed. No one cared how I was feeling or what I wanted. I wanted my baby. So I threw myself into work at the roller disco. I was still living in the flat with Joe.

5. Second Baby, Second Chance

About two months after Christmas I was feeling sick and tired and had put on weight. Joe asked me what was wrong with me. When I went to the doctor it turned out that I was pregnant again. I was so happy, I couldn't believe it. We went for a scan. I was five months pregnant and hadn't known, and there's me working in a roller disco flying around on a pair of roller blades! Joe and I had a long chat and we agreed to give it another go. I agreed only on the condition that we moved. I wanted to go back to Ireland. I needed to be near Kelly; I had to see her and be around her, it was the only way I could cope. Joe agreed and the move was on. We sold everything in our place and left for Ireland. I couldn't wait to be near Kelly again. I was happier than I'd been in a while. We found a flat in Sandycove, a bedsit near the beach, and Joe got a job.

I am more content. We are getting on better, Joe and I, and I am able to see Kelly. She is a year old now and walking. She's so cute. The adoption hasn't been mentioned. I try not to think about it. Maybe it won't happen. Maybe when they see that Joe and I are getting on better they'll change their minds.

I am getting big now and can feel the baby moving. I'm looking forward to having the baby. This is the second chance that I wanted so badly. I've started to spend time with my Uncle Des and Aunt Alice who have moved to Greystones. I am getting to know them better.

We were always told, when we were children, that they hated us and didn't want us around. But I knew different because when I babysat for them they were always good to me and made me feel welcome. Now, as an adult myself, I'm enjoying spending time with them.

We don't know when the new baby is due exactly as my periods weren't happening after the beating, so I'm getting plenty of scans and check-ups. I'm tired all the time though. It turns out I'm anaemic again. They're concerned in the hospital so they've decided to start labour early. I'm given a date to go in. I'm excited but nervous too.

Joe and I stayed in Bray in my parents' house the night before I was to go into hospital. I got up the next morning and got the bus to Loughlinstown Hospital on my own. I can't remember why, I think Joe had to work. They induced me. I was in labour all day. I was on my own for most of it, apart from a nurse coming in every now and then. I had my baby girl that evening. It was 24 June 1986. Again I was overwhelmed with feelings of love for her. I decided to call her Kristel because it reminded me of my sister Christine. Joe came in to the hospital that night to see us and he was happy too. I felt it was a new start for us. I was hopeful that we could still be a happy family.

Joe remained in my parents' house in Bray while I was in hospital for a week. What I didn't know was that my mother was telling him awful stories about me, what a bitch I was as a child and how I tried to wreck her marriage. I couldn't believe Joe would listen to her, the stuff she said was dirty and vile. My Uncle Des came in to collect me and Kristel from the hospital. He brought me to their house for dinner before I went home. They made me feel so welcome and asked if I was OK, whether I needed anything. My Aunt Alice was very good to me. I was growing very close to them.

Kristel was a great baby and I loved being a mother. It wasn't going to be taken away from me this time, I vowed. Our bedsit was small now that we had Kristel. It was also very damp. We talked about moving to Bray. I wanted Kristel and Kelly close so that they could grow up together. In my head Kelly was still very much my daughter too and I dearly wanted to be part of her life.

About three months later we organized for Kristel to be christened. My mother said we could have the party in her house after the church as we couldn't have people in our bedsit, it was too small and cramped. We agreed and asked a few friends. Austin and his partner had a baby girl as well. She was born five weeks after Kristel. They had decided to return to live in Ireland too. The christening went well and we had a good time. Christine said we should all go out that night and I wanted to. I hadn't been out for ages but Joe didn't like the idea. He turned nasty and he went to hit me. I decided we were over. On the night of Kristel's christening we broke up. I left the bedsit the day after and got a flat in Bray while Joe stayed there.

I was on my own but I didn't care. I had Kristel. After about six months Joe told me he was moving back to England but would keep in touch to see Kristel.

I was doing OK on my own. Christine would come and stay from time to time, keeping me company and helping out. Laura at this stage had gone with a guy to live in England. Richard would come and stay with me quite a bit too and babysit for me. When Kristel's first birthday was approaching I decided to have a party for her as Joe said he was coming over from England to see her. My mam and dad were taking the moral high ground and wouldn't have him near Kelly now because of his violence and criminal record (back in England he had ended up in prison a second time). I didn't care as long as I could see her. I took Kristel to the ferry to meet Joe. He didn't arrive. I was so upset. What a birthday for Kristel – no party, no sign or word from her dad. That was it for me, I didn't want to speak to him again. I resolved to stay on my own. I would get my life together myself.

Kelly was almost two and I was twenty when my parents presented the adoption papers for me to sign. They'd arranged everything from their end. All that was needed was my signature. I was back to square one at the time, with a young baby and no partner. Trying to care for her on my own, trying to make ends meet. I was never interviewed by anyone from the Adoption Board. No official from any State department ever spoke to me about having my baby adopted. I hadn't a clue what the proper procedures were. I was supposed to take the papers to someone called a 'commissioner for oaths' and have my signature witnessed and the papers stamped. My mother kept up the pressure on me to do that. I didn't know what a commissioner for oaths was but I remembered seeing a sign outside a door on a street in Bray. The office was situated upstairs over a shop. I made an appointment to see him. I wasn't there long enough that day to sit down. He explained nothing to me. He just witnessed my signature, stamped the papers and took the money.

Looking out the window, I saw my parents with Kelly. They were standing across the road waiting for me. My mother was making sure I'd gone through with it. I had. I had signed over my child to my parents.

Years later I wondered how it could be that they were allowed to do that without anyone official consulting me. Surely more than my signature was required? Surely someone from the Adoption Board should have contacted me to double-check that I was giving up my child of my own volition? That I wasn't being coerced into it? Didn't they have a responsibility to do that? I may not have been pressured into it but I was very young and was in a bad place emotionally and mentally at the time, incapable, I believe, as a result of my abuse, of making rational decisions. It torments me to this day that my parents were able to organize the adoption of my child with no official involvement. I have since wondered if the adoption was even legal, the way it was done.

I met another guy and fell for him. For the first time I was really, genuinely happy, and he loved Kristel. My twenty-first birthday was coming up and Paul[2] organized drinks for me in a local pub. My aunties and uncles turned up, but not my mam and dad. It made him turn against them, that and other things – how my mother spoke to me, the bitchy things she said, keeping Kelly at a distance from me so I couldn't cuddle her or do things for her. She also tried to

2 Not his real name.

keep Kristel and Kelly apart but they were kids and loved playing together.

I became so close to Paul. I brought him with me to the wedding when Austin got married. We got engaged. We went to meet his mother, who lived in England. I didn't tell Paul about my abuse. Just as I'd kept it from Joe, I was trying to suppress it, not wanting even to think about it to myself.

Paul and I were together for about a year when I found out I was pregnant again. When I told him he wasn't happy. He went on the drink. After about two weeks of him sulking he arrived at my flat, drunk. Boy was I angry. I didn't drink myself and wouldn't have it around Kristel. We had a row. It was around Easter time because he brought Easter eggs for Kristel but he was so angry he smashed them. I went mad; I wasn't having that in front of Kristel and I told him to get out, that we were finished. I didn't mean it but my head was all over the place, worrying about another baby.

Christine found out she was pregnant too. It brought us closer now that we had something in common. She was still living at home.

I was trying my best but I felt down a lot of the time. I worried about how I was going to cope on my own with two babies. Kristel brought me so much joy and love and most of all she needed me. Now another baby would be needing me, but it would be a struggle on my own. What would I do for money? Then I heard that Paul was seeing someone else, which really hurt. I truly thought he loved me.

I would lie awake at night in the flat on my own, hurt and worried, everything churning around in my mind – past, present and future – and it was getting harder for me to function.

6. Confronting My Past

The date for my first prenatal appointment came up. The maternity wing at Loughlinstown Hospital, which was nearest and where I had Kristel, had closed at that time and so I was going to Holles Street Hospital in the middle of the city instead. I had been feeling down and was very depressed on the day I went. I was being taken through my medical history, being asked about having Kelly and Kristel, when I broke down. The nurse became alarmed. She called a social worker to come talk to me. She put me in a private room to wait. The social worker arrived and asked me some questions. What did I do? I blurted it all out about my abuse. Here I was – twenty-one, nearly twenty-two – and I was telling the first person, ever, about it. The social worker spoke with me for a bit and said she would get in touch with social workers in Bray about me. On the bus on the way home I felt very scared yet I was relieved that I had finally told someone about it, someone 'official'. I didn't know how to handle how I felt though. All kinds of mixed emotions were churning inside me. Relief that the burden had been lifted off me, guilt and shame that now others knew about this awful, private thing that I'd kept hidden for so long.

About a week later a social worker from Bray got in touch with me. She asked me to go into the Bray office. I nearly didn't go but things were getting so bad, the things I was thinking so awful that in the end I plucked up the courage to go.

I missed Paul badly. I wrote him a letter asking him to give me another chance, that I was scared of having another baby on my own. When I'd heard he was seeing someone else I thought it was just a casual thing. That is until his new girlfriend came to my door holding the letter I'd written, telling me to leave her boyfriend alone and saying that he wasn't the father of the baby I was carrying. Boy did I feel stupid for writing that letter. Humiliated. It hurt so much.

The more I hurt the more I think of my past. About being continuously abused by my father. The almost nightly routine of being called to make him coffee, his signal to me to come to be abused. I think about the times I was taken out of the house, to dark lay-bys at night, to the beach, the golf course, the cemetery. I'm overwhelmed by it, realizing now just how often it happened. So I've begun talking to the social worker. She is asking the right questions and I'm giving her all the answers. I'm telling her all about my past. She asks me about my brothers and sisters, if they were abused also. I don't think so but the truth is I don't really know. Would my father have stopped at me? It leads me to tell Christine about my abuse and ask her if she too was subjected to it. She says no.

I was seeing the social worker every week at that time. I was still so lonely. I was also visiting my parents and still seeing Kelly. When I was about six months pregnant I was allocated a council house in Bray. It was in Oldcourt, the same estate where my mam and dad lived, about ten doors away from them. It might seem contradictory that I wanted to live near them, but I needed to be close so I could see

Kelly all the time and have some part in her life. It also meant that Kristel could play with her sister. I wanted my two daughters to be close.

One day before I moved I had a massive row with my mother in her house. It was over Richard. He was her pet. We were upstairs. She turned nasty on me, shouting and screaming. I went down the stairs and into the kitchen. She was lashing out at me. I shoved her because Kristel was on the ground and my mother nearly trod on her, and Kelly was watching it all. I put Kristel in her buggy and went to leave. My mother was still shouting, saying that I had ruined her marriage, that I was sleeping with my father. As I walked out there was a neighbour standing there listening. I was mortified. I burned with shame; the kids and neighbours listening. I cried hard all the way back to my flat.

When I told my social worker about the row, she asked me why I had left, why I hadn't just said, 'Yes he was sleeping with me.' I couldn't answer. The shame was so bad. I promised myself that next time I would.

I got busy moving to the house in Oldcourt. I was so happy to have been housed by the council. I would at least have a stable home for myself and my kids. Being able to see Kelly kept me going. I was able to just walk over the few doors to her. My mam and dad fussed over Christine being pregnant, buying her stuff, but they didn't help me. I didn't hear from Paul either.

I buried how I was feeling about the abuse from one visit with the social worker to the next. I was learning to compartmentalize it.

I got on with things. Christine was due to have her baby in November and I was due shortly afterwards. She went into labour and we all went to the hospital, my mam and dad and me. We sat in the waiting room for hours and hours. My mother would go in and out, telling us what a hard time she was having. We stayed there most of the night until her baby girl was born. The next day we went back in to visit with balloons and cards. The following day Christine came home. I went with my dad to collect her and her baby. Coming back I started to get pains. I nearly had to ask my dad to turn back. That night I cleaned the house and organized Kristel so things would be ready for me going in to hospital. The next morning, after a bad night, I walked across to my mam and dad's house. The neighbours were in looking at Christine's baby. I told my mam to call the ambulance as the baby was coming. I sat in the kitchen in labour while they all stayed in the sitting room admiring the baby.

A neighbour came and sat with me to wait for the ambulance. She had asked where I was and my mother had said, 'She's in the kitchen in labour.'

The ambulance driver asked if anyone was coming with me and they told him 'no'. At the hospital I felt lonely. Apart from the doctors and nurses checking in on me I lay there for hours on my own. I had such a sense of déjà vu.

That evening, on 16 November 1988, my son, Patrick Austin, was born. He was 10 lb 1 oz. Why I called him after my father I will never know. The next day I rang Paul to tell him I had a boy and he told me he didn't want to know and that he wasn't the father. I felt crushed. I suppose I had harboured some hope that he would come round when the baby was born.

7. Happiness and Heartbreak

We are in the sitting room watching a film I've rented. It's a children's film really but we're all watching it, Kristel, Tony[3] and me. The baby is on my lap, lying back contentedly, nearly asleep with his head tucked under my chin. I can feel Tony's shoulder, warm, up against mine. I feel so happy. I'm happy that I have found this man and that he loves me and my kids and I love him. He's content to stay in with us on a Saturday night. He likes taking us out too. We're like a proper family.

Richard was going out with a girl and they'd babysit for me from time to time so a few days after Christmas – 29 December – I had gone out for the first time since having Patrick. I was twenty-two. That night I met Tony. God, I couldn't keep my eyes off him, he was lovely. He asked me to meet him the following week. I couldn't believe my luck. That week couldn't pass quickly enough. I was really excited. He had a good job, was from a nice area and had a good family background. He seemed to be well out of my league. But he kept asking me out after that first date and we soon fell in love. Tony adored my kids and was happy to spend nights in with us and to take us on outings at weekends. I don't think it went down too well when he told his mam and dad he had met a girl bringing up two kids.

We've been going together for six weeks. They've been six of the best weeks of my life. Now Tony has taken me out for the evening.

---

3 Not his real name.

'We have to talk,' he says. Anxiety builds up inside me. I feel sick. He drives us to the beach in Shankill. I am quiet and nervous, thinking he is going to finish with me. I resign myself to it. Promising myself I won't cry in front of him. He parks the car, turns off the engine, turns to me. Clears his throat. Here it comes. 'Will you marry me, Fiona?' he asks. What a shock! He wants me! I feel the anxiety leave my body, draining away like water down a plughole. Now a warm feeling of happiness is washing over me as what he's said sinks in. I smile. Then I laugh. 'Yes! Yes, yes, yes, yes, yes!' I am over the moon with joy.

A week or two later Christine announced that her boyfriend had asked her to marry him too. My mam and dad thought he was the best thing because he was in the army. Tony and I set a date, 29 December 1989, a year to the day we met. Christine and her fiancé set their date for 21 November, my mam and dad's twenty-fifth wedding anniversary. They agreed between them that mam and dad would renew their wedding vows after Christine's wedding ceremony. I shook my head in disbelief when I heard that. Their rows were as bad as ever. I thought that my mother might be trying to impress the neighbours.

I was still talking to the social worker about my past. I decided that I had to tell Tony. I had to be honest with him, to let him know what he was marrying. We talked a lot as I was worried about getting married after having two failed relationships. I was also concerned about him taking on the responsibility of my children. Tony would write me beautiful love letters to reassure me though. He also wanted to put his name on Patrick's birth certificate when I went to register his birth but I said no because that would make my children different. He agreed that we should wait until we were married and he would legally adopt them both.

My mother and father spent all their time helping Christine organize her wedding and they paid for it. They went to buy her dress with her. I was getting on well with Tony's mam and dad at that stage, they seemed to have warmed to me, and they tried to help me as much as they could because they knew I wasn't getting any help from my parents. Tony's mother even came with me to get my dress as the wedding got closer. All of the excitement in my family was about Christine's wedding, and her day went very well.

It's a week before my wedding. It's late at night, about eleven o'clock. Tony has gone home and I've come over to my parents' house. My mother and I are in the sitting room. We're talking about Kristel and how she is being a handful to manage. 'You're not hard enough on her, you should give her a beating when she's like that,' she tells me. I look at her in shock. 'No way,' I hear myself say, 'I would never rear my kids the way we were brought up.' She gets annoyed at that and starts going on about me wrecking her marriage.

'What do you mean?' I ask her. 'Sleeping with your father,' she says. I look at her. 'You believe that, do you?' She says, 'Yes, it's true, isn't it?' Well I start getting brave and say, 'Yes, it is.' It's her turn to be shocked. I've never said that back to her before. I start to shake. I can't believe I've blurted it out. My mother gets up from the chair and goes upstairs, shouting at my father who is in bed. 'You were sleeping with her, she's just admitted it.' I phone Tony in a panic, crying at what I've done.

The next day I didn't see anyone. Tony came and took me to his mam and dad's and I spent Christmas there with the kids. None of my family spoke to me all week after that and my wedding was getting closer. I didn't know if my father was going to be giving me away as we'd planned. I can't understand now why I would have wanted him to.

My big day arrived. I was so nervous. I was in bits. The limousine arrived to take me to the church and then, finally, my father showed up. I was relieved. He didn't speak to me on the way to the church, St Fergal's in Ballywaltrim, Bray. Thank God it was only a five-minute journey. During the wedding Mass, when we had to offer each other the sign of peace, I had to turn and shake hands with my mother and father but they turned away from me. People noticed something was going on. The wedding continued but the tension was really bad.

At the end of the reception, when the guests were to say goodbye to the bride and groom, my mother again refused to have anything to do with me. An aunt caught me crying and asked me what was going on. I couldn't tell her. Tony took me outside and I cried my eyes out. He was so angry that they'd stopped talking to me and spoiled my wedding day.

The social worker keeps on at me about my situation. She has been working on getting me moved from Oldcourt so I won't be so close to my parents but she knows it will take time. She thinks it's a bad thing that I am living so near to them. She keeps on at me to make a statement to the gardaí. I feel hassled by her. Like I'm being backed into a corner. Tony is doing his best to support me but I sense that it's getting hard for him. I can tell. Starting married life wasn't easy for us with so much going against us. Here we are, a month after the wedding, and

I've just found out I'm pregnant. Then there is the stress of moving house again. The houses on the Oldcourt estate are being refurbished by the council and I am being moved to number 16. My parents are being moved to number 66, so we will still be living in the same estate, though further away from each other.

We bought things for the new house in Oldcourt out of the money we got as wedding presents and it is looking nice. Tony got a company car. But the hassle keeps coming.

One day we were out with my uncle and aunt, Des and Alice. I'd become even closer to them at that stage. I invited them back to ours for tea. As we pulled up outside the house my mother and father walked past and she shouted, 'There she is, the whore and the whore's master.' Des turned to her and said, 'Breda, will you stop that, she's your daughter.' Tony and I got Kristel and Patrick into the house as quickly as we could so they wouldn't hear what was being said. Alice also walked in, shocked at what she'd heard. I was fighting back the tears and shame.

When Des and Alice left I had a good cry to Tony. We talked and he asked me to tell Des and Alice the truth. I did and they didn't seem shocked, but Des got very upset. He told me that many years ago when I was little my mother had got a beating from my dad and went to my nanny's and she told Des at that time that she thought my father was sleeping with me. Des went to challenge my father but he denied it, saying my mother was such a troublemaker and a liar. Of course Des knew what my mother was like and the trouble she could cause with her lies so he believed my father and walked away. Poor Des, he felt so guilty about that he cried and hugged me, saying how sorry he was. Des and Alice then told the rest of my aunts and uncles about my abuse.

The social worker is still on at me to talk to the gardaí and finally I agree to. I don't really want to but I'm so worried about Kelly, especially now that I'm not going to be as close by to keep an eye on her. She is being raised in a house where a paedophile lives. I cannot deny that reality. I remember the promise I made, the night she was born, to protect her always. I have to make good on that promise. A meeting is set up with the gardaí.

The social worker also gives me the name of a psychologist to see and tells me he'll help me deal with my feelings and prepare me to speak to the gardaí. I go to see him. I don't like him at first. He seems offhand, a bit distant. I find it hard to talk to him. He is making me remember things I don't want to.

What I didn't notice while all this was going on was that Tony wasn't handling it very well. Not that I was a saint or anything. I was demanding so much reassurance, my moods were up and down, and I was sick too, being pregnant. Tony threw himself into his football and wasn't around much. One night I was so sick the hospital wanted me to go in and I had to wait until he finished football training to take me. When the nurse asked why I took so long to get there, I told her and she went mad at Tony, asking him why football was more important than his wife and child. It kind of wasn't fair on him, I felt. He was putting up with so much.

Things moved on and I was taken into Holles Street Hospital because my blood-sugar levels were not right. They knew I was having a big baby. He was 10 lb 7 oz, born on 14

August 1990. Lewis George. Tony picked the name Lewis. We were delighted with our new baby. Tony came into the hospital with flowers and an eternity ring for me. Lewis took his mind off things for a while but, as things settled, all our troubles came flooding back.

I'm back seeing the social worker and the psychologist too. Tony and I are struggling on but the cracks are showing. We are arguing more. I just want things to be right. For us to be a normal family. Why can't that be? My abuse is to blame, I think, as I lie beside him in bed at night. It's too much for him to handle. It's followed me all my life and now it's going to ruin the one good thing I've ever had. I cry quietly, turning into the pillow so he won't wake.

We continued on for about seven or eight months more. During that time I made enquiries about having my Fallopian tubes tied. Because of the problems I'd had with the pregnancy, I didn't want to risk having any more children. I had had varicose veins from a young age so it wasn't medically advisable for me to take the pill. Now I decided I wanted a permanent solution. We'd talked it over and Tony supported my decision. I would have to go before a board at Holles Street Hospital to make my case.

After a row one night Tony told me he was leaving me. He packed his clothes and said he just needed space. So off he went to his mother and father's. I didn't hear anything for a few days until his mother called and I told her I needed money. Two days later I was struggling to cope on my own and burned my hand, scalding it when I wasn't paying attention. I wasn't sleeping or eating, missing Tony and worrying about us.

His dad dropped off some money. It annoyed me. I

wanted to talk to my husband. Finally, one night he came round. We chatted and ended up in bed together but he didn't stay the night. He said he had to get home. I was so hurt by that. Wasn't his home with me?

His father called round the next day and gave out to me for sleeping with Tony. God, I was so embarrassed, my father-in-law standing in my home having a go at me for sleeping with my husband. I just stood there and took it. I felt so humiliated.

I was notified to go before the board of Holles Street Hospital about having my tubes tied. I attended and gave my reasons for wanting the procedure. They refused, however, on the grounds of my young age and the fact that I was now separated.

Tony's brother was due to get married and Kristel was to be a flower girl, so about a week later Tony came to collect us and take us to his mother's house for Kristel to get fitted for her dress. He went off to football and left us there. We went upstairs so Kristel could try on the dress and we were in the room Tony was sleeping in. It was a shock for me, seeing his stuff there, his bed and everything. I was missing him so much. I really loved him.

When he came back after football he brought a big wedding present downstairs to give to his brother, one I supposed was to be from him and me. I asked him what it was and he said it was a microwave. His mother then piped up and said, 'Yeah, I went with Tony to pick it out.' I felt so cut out. She was doing my job. Like a fool I started to cry. I couldn't take much more.

When Tony saw I was getting upset he asked me to go for

a drive, so we left the kids with his mam and went off. I'm not sure where we went, my mind was in such a tizzy, but he told me he was thinking of coming back that evening, but after seeing me so upset he decided he couldn't do it, and he told me we were finished. I was falling to bits. We went to get the kids and he said he didn't want to leave me back at the house alone; he would take me to Des and Alice's house. So that's where we went.

So many things were going on in my head. I'd failed again. I couldn't keep a husband or a marriage. I was good for nothing; my kids would be better off without me.

I'm in the kitchen in Des and Alice's house. Tony has gone inside to the sitting room to talk to Des. I am so tired. I can't sleep though, I'm too upset. Everything Tony said is going around and around in my head. I look up and see a bottle of paracetamol. I keep looking at the bottle. Before I know it I'm picking it up and swallowing handfuls of tablets. I take all I can. Tony comes back out to the kitchen with Des and tells me he'll drop me home. We go out and get into the car. I'm feeling woozy. I'm sleepy too. My brain feels like it's full of fog but through it I realize that, if he drops me home, my kids will be the ones that will find me. I don't want that. I tell him what I've done. I can't keep my eyes open. I just want to give up. He starts shouting at me. He turns the car around, says he's driving back to Des and Alice's. He tells them what I've done. Poor Des and Alice. So shocked and upset. They'll mind my kids while he takes me to the hospital. I pass out.

I came round in the hospital. I felt awful. The doctors wanted to pump my stomach but I wouldn't let them. I really wanted to die. I was no good for anything and I wouldn't be a good mother either. I kept passing in and out of consciousness, but I kept saying no. I don't know how long we were there but the next thing I can remember was Tony calling me names, a bitch, saying I was selfish doing that to him, saying loads of things like that when no one was around. I wasn't talking, just crying so much. I wanted it all to stop. I wanted the pain inside me to end. The doctors and nurses kept coming back, wanting to pump my stomach. I kept refusing to let them. I just wasn't worth the hassle.

Every time they left Tony called me more names. It was getting worse. I don't know what kicked in but I got angry and thought, 'I'm not leaving my kids with you, you asshole.' The doctor came in and said that all my aunts, uncles and cousins were outside and that he would let them hold me down to pump my stomach if I didn't agree, so I did, but more out of anger at Tony. I was adamant that I wasn't leaving my kids to be reared by him. My stomach was pumped and I was moved to the Intensive Care Unit as they didn't know what damage I'd done to my liver with the paracetamol. I woke the next day and was sorry I was alive. Things just seemed so bleak. I couldn't talk to anyone. I just lay in bed, feeling a complete and utter failure.

Tony's mother came to see me. She went on about trying to get on with things; that my marriage was gone and I needed to get sorted. I just lay there so depressed when she left the hospital. I got the social worker to come and speak to me. I hadn't eaten anything since they'd pumped my stomach, and they were worried. I told the hospital social worker about the other social worker I was seeing and about seeing the psychologist. God, I was a nut job. The second day a priest came to see me. My mother-in-law had asked him to come and talk to me. Well, he went on and on, telling me not to give up on my marriage, that marriage was for life. God, was I not confused enough? I wasn't the one who wanted out of the marriage. It was all too much to handle.

Tony came to see me this morning. It's my third day in ICU. He tells me he has emptied the house of his stuff, that we are finished, there's no going back. He feels it's better this way, clearing his belongings from the house while I'm in hospital. He offers to pick me up when I'm discharged and drop me home. I think I'm being discharged tomorrow. The psychologist has rung me and made arrangements to see me as well as the social worker. Tony says he'll take me. My kids are still at Des and Alice's house.

The next day at my aunt and uncle's house it felt as if Tony couldn't wait to get out of there. Then, what a shock it was going back to the house and seeing all his things gone, no trace of him left. He did a good job clearing the place. I sat in that house that night and cried. I slept on the sofa; I couldn't go to the bed that had been our bed. I cried and cried like he'd died, which I guess, in a way, he had. The Tony I knew had died.

8. My First Complaint to the Gardaí

It was just me and the kids now. With Des and Alice's help and support I began to get myself together. We had no money and I had to go to the social welfare office. They told me they would give me money but I had to come back with a court date for maintenance from Tony.

I enrolled my children in a playschool. It was part of a family support centre and was run by the Irish Society for the Prevention of Cruelty to Children. It was for children having problems, and mine did have problems; they missed Tony so much. The playschool was a great help and they put me in touch with a group of women that would meet up to support each other in going to court for custody rights, maintenance and other family law matters. It was organized by the women's refuge. They got me a solicitor as well. He was based in Bray and worked for the refuge free of charge. He was such a good man. In the meantime I kept going to the psychologist. I had begun to warm to him. The social worker got me a home help to come and mind the kids for me so that I could keep seeing the psychologist. And, after thinking about it for so long, I finally made a statement to the gardaí about my abuse.

I'm doing it. At last. A female garda is here in my house, taking a statement from me about the abuse. The social worker is here with me too. I've been so nervous about doing this. I still am. I've gone back and forth with it in my mind so many times. Now I'm worried about not saying things in the right order, because I remember different things from different times. I've a sick feeling in my stomach. I feel sweaty. I still can't remember a lot of stuff but I do the best I can. I want to fit in as much as possible.

The social worker tells me not to worry, that the garda will come back if she needs to clarify any of the details in my statement. The garda is nice to me. Still, it's hard to tell what I've now come to think of as my Big Dirty Secret.

I got a court date for the maintenance matter. When it came Tony was ordered to pay me £125 a week. Afterwards he said he wanted custody of Lewis. That came as a terrible shock. I hadn't expected it and couldn't believe it. Things were going from bad to worse. I was determined to fight it though, there was no way he was getting my son. No way anyone would ever take a child from me again. We went back to court. My solicitor told me Tony was using my abuse against me to say I was an unfit mother. That cut me to the bone. What a low blow. I had worked very hard to be the best mother I could to my children. I had hidden the abuse deep inside me so that it wouldn't affect them. I decided that if Tony got custody I would run away with the kids.

The night before the court case, after I put the children to bed, my sitting-room window came crashing in. Other windows in the house were broken too. I blamed it on members of my family. I thought they did it because they were upset and annoyed that I'd spoken to the gardaí about my abuse. I knew that the gardaí had paid my parents a visit on foot of my complaint.

The timing with the broken windows was awful. How

could I say in court I was a good mother when I didn't even have basic things like glass in my windows? The home help was sent to me so that I could attend court. I kissed my kids goodbye. It was so hard, not knowing what was going to happen. Des and Alice came with me for support. I was very grateful to them.

My solicitor was great and he was able to work out a deal with Tony's solicitor. The custody claim was dropped. I agreed to drop the amount I was getting in maintenance to £75 a week.

Tony came over that afternoon and took the kids out for a few hours. I didn't want him at the house, seeing the windows all boarded up. I was embarrassed. When he came back he sat in the car while his mother came to the door and told me that he had decided he didn't want to see the kids again, that I was to contact her if I wanted anything from him, and not to contact him directly.

Afterwards I got my solicitor to send a letter to Tony's mother, telling her to stay out of my business. I was lashing out in anger, I knew, but I couldn't help it. I was so upset, frustrated and hurt. I had gotten on well with Tony's parents and felt that we'd grown close and that they had come to like me even though at the outset they weren't happy that Tony was going out with someone who had children. I felt betrayed when they turned against me.

Finally I am standing up to my mother-in-law. All my visits to the psychologist are paying off. I'm learning things about myself. Like not telling people when I am hurt, always putting a front on. Why my make-up is so important to me, so that people can't see the real me. I learned to keep things deep inside while I was growing up. I was an expert at hiding the abuse. With the help of the psychologist I am starting to understand myself better.

In September 1991 I got a letter from the Dublin Regional Marriage Tribunal asking me to attend a meeting about my marriage at the Diocesan Offices at Archbishop's House, Drumcondra, Dublin. The letter was from a Fr Churchill, the Judicial Vicar at the Dublin Regional Marriage Tribunal. He wanted to see me because Tony wanted our marriage annulled.

I was shocked and so hurt. He wanted our marriage to be erased, as if it had never happened?

My first considerations were practical ones: who would mind the children and how would I get to Dublin? I wasn't driving at that time. I didn't even know how to get to Drumcondra. A girl at the playschool offered to drive me while the staff there minded the kids. And so I went in, not knowing what to expect.

I was ill at ease and anxious. I am not sure who I talked to that day. I thought it was the archbishop but, having thought about it, I believe it must have been Fr Churchill as all subsequent correspondence came from him. I'm sure whoever it was introduced themselves to me that day but I cannot remember the name.

This person, whoever he was, put a recorder on the table to tape our conversation. I was nervous anyway and that made me even more so. Why hadn't I brought someone in with me for support?

He started to explain to me that Tony wanted an annulment. I was told it could be granted in special circumstances.

As I understood it, an annulment means a marriage is deemed to have never happened. 'How can you say that,' I asked, 'when I had a child?' He wanted the names of the people who were witnesses to our marriage. He asked deeply personal questions about our sex life and if we'd had sex before marriage. I was mortified. I was blushing. I stammered and stuttered. Then he asked me to submit myself for psychological assessment. I was even asked to sign a note pledging to pay the £90 fee for the psychologist when I had the money. The cheek! I got quite angry and asked if he thought it was OK for the Church to condone a man walking out on his family and for them then to get me in to try to cancel my marriage? How dare they? I said, fighting back tears. Annulling my marriage would make our child illegitimate in the Church's eyes yet that's what they were going to facilitate.

When I was asked to see a psychologist, I guessed that Tony was making his case for annulment on the grounds that I was unstable as a result of my sexual abuse. The suicide attempt would have bolstered his case. My abuse was being used against me. It wasn't the first time and it wouldn't be the last.

I walked out and I vowed I would never again have anything to do with the Church. *They lie, they ram religion down my throat and then tell me they can make my marriage go away as if it never happened. I don't care, they will never get me back in there. They can give him his annulment but they will do it without any help from me.* In any case, as I understood it, the State doesn't recognize annulment.

They wrote to me a few times after that meeting but I

73

never responded. It dragged on for several years. The day I went to Drumcondra I had signed a release allowing the tribunal to contact my social worker. Fr Churchill wrote to her in May 1995 and she replied the following month. While I wasn't privy to his letter, and so don't know what he asked, I do have a copy of the reply she sent him. In it she outlines the ongoing contact she had had with me and said it had to do with difficulties in relationships with my parents and boyfriends arising out of my sexual abuse by my father.

She said she had general concerns, when I told her I was getting married, about my ability to form a healthy relationship with any man because of the damage done to me by the sexual abuse committed by my father and my parents' rejection of me. She said too that while she'd had virtually no direct contact with Tony she believed my needs were too great to be met by him and that he wasn't strong enough or mature enough to meet those needs and keep the family together.

I only got a copy of the social worker's letter in 2012 when the Health Service Executive released my files to me. The content of the social worker's letter, in response to Fr Churchill's enquiries, confirmed to me that my instincts back then had been right all along. The Church was happy to follow the agenda Tony had set out for them, as I had believed back then. On the day I was interviewed at Archbishop's House the line of questioning made me feel very much as if I were the person in the wrong. I didn't get any sense that the Church wanted to tease out the facts and make an unbiased determination on our marriage. Whatever happened to the sanctity of marriage, I wondered? The Church didn't appear to think it was sanctified in my case.

Tony got his annulment in November 1997, some six years after I had that meeting in Drumcondra. In the eyes of the Church, Lewis and I had been erased. The copy of the Decree of Nullity of Marriage that I received had the following condition written on it: *The Respondent, Fiona O'Brien, may not enter a future marriage in the Catholic Church, until she has assured the local Ordinary of her due preparedness for Christian Marriage.* Tony has since remarried.

I've never been particularly religious. Other than First Communion and Confirmation we weren't taken to Mass much growing up. It never dawned on me to seek solace in prayer as a child when I was being sexually, physically and emotionally abused. Perhaps, in my isolation, I felt God too had turned his back on me. Certainly the annulment business soured me for ever with the Catholic Church.

When I first learned about Tony's plans to have our marriage annulled, it was a really difficult time. Somehow, and from somewhere, I found the strength to keep going. The people at the playschool were very good to me. Coming up to Christmas 1991 I had no tree. I couldn't afford one. The school dropped one off to me. The women's refuge sent me a hamper of food, and one of Tony's friends arrived with loads of toys for the kids. People's kindness was amazing.

I went to Des and Alice's for our first Christmas alone. It was also my second wedding anniversary. People were worried about me but I wasn't going to sink so low again that I'd hurt myself after fighting to keep my kids. No way.

I got word from the council that they were moving me to a house in a different estate in Bray. It was in Heatherwood, on the Boghall Road. I had mixed feelings about the move. On the one hand I knew that moving away from my parents was the right thing to do. On the other it meant I would see less of Kelly. Getting me moved was the last thing my social worker did for me because she got transferred in February 1993. That old feeling of being let down returned. I had come to trust her.

My money was sorted at least; I used to have to walk to the courthouse in Bray on Fridays at about five o'clock. It closed at 5.15 p.m. Tony's dad would come and pay my maintenance in; the courthouse would then give me a cheque. I'd do my grocery shopping and rush home before it was delivered. In hail, rain or snow, dark nights, every Friday I did that. What kept me going as I pushed Kristel, Patrick and Lewis in the buggy was swearing to myself that I would learn how to drive. And at least I had the children.

Some months after I'd started going to see him, the psychologist told me he was moving on too. So that was it. I never got anyone else. I kept in with the women's refuge group and made friends with other mothers of children in the playschool. I did the cooking in the school two mornings a week. In doing so I was trying in some small way to repay the kindness that was shown to me.

Tony's mother would come to the playschool to see Lewis. She would do this every six months or so. I didn't

want her in my home so the playschool allowed us to use a
room for the visits. Tony was never spoken about.

*I was at home earlier today, doing housework and listening to the
radio. The news came on. The main story was about a nightwatchman
being murdered in Dun Laoghaire Yacht Club. I stopped to listen,
shocked by the news. He was an elderly man. It had happened in the
course of a robbery. He'd been beaten to death with a length of timber.
How awful. It was terrible, I thought, the poor man.*

*Little did I know then that Richard was involved. I've been told the
news, just now, by my parents. My little brother, who I had practically
reared, who had babysat for me, has killed a man. Oh God. It is so,
so shocking.*

Richard was twenty-one at the time. A friend of his was
caught with him. There was outrage from people locally
about the killing and I couldn't blame them. I didn't go to
any of my brother's court appearances or the court case in
which he was convicted of manslaughter and sentenced to
ten years in prison. His friend was also convicted.

Life at that time wasn't good. If it hadn't been for Des
and Alice and their kids, who gave us the family we needed,
that my kids needed, it would have been much worse. They
have been so good to us, such a support over the years. I
tried getting on with my life. I did some courses in parent-
ing and continued to help with the cooking at the playschool.
I hadn't heard anything back from the gardaí after making
that first statement.

I still used the same shops and I would sometimes see my
parents and sisters, but they would just pass me by. It had
been like that since I'd made my complaint to the gardaí. My

relatives had heard about it from my parents and some of my dad's family contacted me, an uncle and aunt, and I told them what had happened to me. I'm not sure if they believed me but they did listen. It was the same with another uncle.

I'm standing here in the hall with my back to the front door. I don't know how long I've been standing here. I can't believe it. Two gardaí have just been at my door. It's been about two years since I made my statement. Out of the blue they called just now. They didn't come in, just stood at the door and told me the DPP has decided not to take the case against my father any further as too much time has passed. I was so shocked and taken aback that all I managed to say was 'OK'. They turned around to leave and I closed the door. I've been standing here since, trying to take it in. So that's it. I'm on my own. I will have to deal with this by myself. I feel so let down.

9. Another Disastrous Relationship

I had to move on. It was a case of sink or swim. I taught myself how to drive in a friend's car and got a job. I saved for and got a car of my own. I was delighted with the freedom it gave me. I would use it for work, making deliveries for a fast-food restaurant, but also to get around in and to take my kids on trips and outings. I would often think of Kelly, wanting to see her. One day Kristel told me she and Kelly were doing the Stay Safe Programme in their school. Kelly was a year ahead of Kristel there. It was about nice touches and bad touches, what was appropriate and what was not. I went there and told the principal and class teacher my story so that they would be aware of the abuse perpetrated by my father in whose house Kelly was being reared. I wanted the school to know so that they would keep an eye on her. I'm not sure if the school took me seriously when I told them about my past. I think they thought I was a bit crazy. I told them that Kelly was really my daughter and that Kristel and Kelly were actually sisters. And that part was very believable because they looked so alike people would often confuse them.

Kelly was always on my mind. Her Communion was coming up and I vowed I was going to see her even if I had to stand in the back of the church to do so.

I was out driving in Deansgrange in Dublin one day when

who did I see but my father standing at the bus stop. I stopped the car and asked him if he wanted a lift. God, I was shaking. I honestly can't explain why I stopped; it was just a spur-of-the-moment thing. He accepted my offer and got in the car. He chatted away, asking how I was getting on, how my new house was. It was the first time we'd spoken since I'd made my complaint against him. I asked him if he wanted to call round to the house in Heatherwood for a cup of coffee. I didn't plan it, I don't really know what I was thinking, but I had a friend staying at the house at the time so I felt it was OK. He came to the house. I made him coffee and we talked. It felt surreal, me wondering all the while why I'd invited him to my home and him chatting away as if everything were normal.

He told me he knew that he had ruined my life and that he was sorry. Later he would deny ever having said that. I told him the worst thing I ever did was to let them have Kelly and that he better not touch her.

He told me I could come over to see her, and I did. He and my mother said that I could go to her Communion and I could bring Kristel. I was so happy for Kristel as well as for myself. She didn't know it at the time but she got to attend her older sister's Communion. It was a bittersweet moment for me, my elder daughter making her Holy Communion. It triggered memories of my own.

I have to bury the truth and get on with my life. I have to hide it from the kids. They have no family. I'm thinking: 'If I can bury my past they could have a normal life with normal grandparents, aunts and uncles. We'd be the same as other families. They'd be part of everyday family things.' So I'm trying to do that. I'm back talking to

Christine. I've even been in touch with Richard. I wrote to him in prison. I'm starting to get on with them all again and when memories of the abuse come into my mind I walk out and stay out of their way for a few days, trying to get it out of my head.

Who was I kidding? Only myself. Some days were better than others but at least I was seeing Kelly. We were all having challenges in our lives. We all just got on with things. Me, I went into bad relationships.

I had the coil fitted so that I would at least not have to worry about contraception. It didn't suit me though. I got a massive infection. I had to call out the doctor, it was so bad. He told me I ought to have been in hospital but I couldn't go because there was no one to mind the children. He treated me with antibiotics but my temperature was sky high and he told me I would have to make arrangements for the children so that I could go into hospital the next day if I wasn't any better. The next morning Kristel, who was only about six and a half, helped me get her two brothers ready for playschool. She took them down for me on her way to school. I put a note in one of their pockets, explaining I was ill. Staff at the playschool were concerned when they read the note and they came round to my house. They found me so ill I was unable to get out of bed. They called an ambulance and I was taken to Holles Street Hospital, where they removed the coil. The playschool organized to have the children taken into care for two days while I was there.

Richard was getting through his sentence, being moved from prison to prison. I went to see him a few times. When he came out of prison he got a house in Oldcourt in Bray, the same estate as my mam and dad, Christine and her husband and their in-laws. They were all living in each other's pockets.

My mother never again mentioned me having sex with my father, not after that big row we had before my wedding when the neighbours overheard her shouting at me about it. I guessed she didn't raise it again because I'd had the guts to make a complaint to the gardaí.

Time went by. I had my ups and downs but with Des and Alice's unwavering support I kept going. I even had another baby, a boy, on 30 September 1995. I didn't stay with the father but I didn't care. I wanted more children, they gave me so much love back, it made my life worthwhile. My son's father was a younger guy I'd met. He was around for about a year. I taught him to drive and we got jobs delivering pizzas, sharing my car. In the end he went off with another girl. A short while later I found out I was pregnant. It wasn't an easy pregnancy; I was sick all of the time.

I tried to keep on working. If it hadn't been for friends I wouldn't have coped very well. I called my son Deasún after my Uncle Des. Deasún is Irish for Desmond.

I'm back at work, driving for a takeaway company. I have to do something to make money to provide for us. I bring the kids along with me, the baby strapped into his car seat in the back with the others. I have to take them out with me. I can't afford a babysitter to mind them while I'm working. Besides it means I get to spend the time with them. It's September so the evenings are still bright until late. I try to make it into a game for them, getting them to guess which street we're going to next, guessing which house is getting what, playing I Spy as I drive along. They enjoy it most of the time but they get restless after a while. I chat to them about school as well, as we go, to keep them from being bored. The older children are doing well. Kristel is learning line dancing, she's really keen, and the boys love football.

When Deasún was six weeks old I met another man. I was on a rare night out with a friend when I met a man in a pub and got talking to him. At first I thought Keith[4] was brilliant. He'd been married and had kids. We had a few dates and I fell head over heels with him. I didn't notice that he had a drink problem. He worked all day then headed straight for the pub. He spent Saturdays and Sundays there too, which is where he saw his kids. I'd pick him up at ten o'clock. I didn't see that he wouldn't come to me, that I always had to go and get him.

I also started to hear stories about him being violent to his ex-wife, but there was me, stupid, not listening, believing I was lucky to have got him. Keith loved himself. He dressed up to the nines and was the life and soul of a party. Flirting with other women, making me feel like crap. If I said anything he'd tell me it was all in my head. I was such a fool, believing again that no one would have me with my baby belly.

I've just woken from a dream. I dreamed that Keith had moved in with us. I'd never be on my own again. I lie awake thinking about it, remembering how happy I'd been in the dream. Why did I have to wake? It's not going to happen, I know. He knows how much I love him and want us to be together but Keith won't change for me or for anyone for that matter. He's been staying in my house for weeks now and I decided the other night it was time to ask for money from him for his keep. I'm finding it hard enough to manage on what little money I

4 Not his real name.

have coming in and wanted him to make some contribution. I cooked a meal and went to the pub to collect him. When we got back he sat down to have his dinner, said it was lovely, and I plucked up the courage to ask him to pay his way. He went mad, asked me who I thought I was and said I was lucky to have him. I got a punch in the face. I lost a tooth with the force of the blow. He walked out. I put my finger in my mouth now and feel the hole where my tooth was. I'm embarrassed by it. Now I will have to try to find the money to get it fixed.

It was the first of many blows Keith gave me. I was so scared of being on my own, I put up with it, knowing that, deep down, I wanted and deserved better. I just didn't know how to get it.

I put up with it for a year, us breaking up and getting back together. He even went off with his ex-wife. She rang me to tell me. He knew about my abuse and I think he sensed how vulnerable I was, and that he could get away with the things he did.

I decided to get away myself, get rid of everything and go to England with the kids and start again. I told Keith my decision. I think I was trying to corner him, force him into making a decision to treat me better, to promise he would change for me. My plan was to sell my furniture to get some money behind me and go back to Derby where Laura and her husband and Austin had settled. They were getting on fine. It took about twelve weeks to get ready, selling stuff and packing up.

In that time Keith didn't ask me not to go. He just did the same as always, coming up late after the pub and leaving early the next morning. So I went ahead with my plans. I emptied my house, packed my bags and the children's things and went. Keith came down to the ferry to say goodbye. He bought me a teddy. He cried and I cried. All I wanted was for him to tell me not to go but he didn't.

We arrived in Derby and I rang a phone number for a homeless support agency. I told them I'd left an abusive man and had nowhere to go. They arranged for me and the kids to stay in a bed and breakfast place that night.

I'm looking at my children sleeping. They were exhausted by the time we got here tonight after travelling all day. I feel panicked. What the hell am I doing to them? I realize in dismay that I've taken them away from a settled home, their schools where they were doing well. Their friends. Was I wrong to up and leave the way I did? Is this me again, running away from trouble? Is it always going to be like this? How will we get on here? How will I manage for money? The tears come but I'm trying to cry quietly so as not to wake them. I lean over and rub Deasún's little head. He stirs but doesn't wake. For their sake I have to make this work.

The next day I went to the council and agreed to go into a women's refuge. To my surprise it was actually a lovely place. I had a two-bedroom flat inside a big house that was divided into about twelve flats. I got the kids into schools. I started writing to Keith, telling him how much I loved and missed him. He did the same, sending me cards and love poems. I was so lonely. We were in the refuge for about six weeks when the council gave us a beautiful four-bedroom house. I loved it. The day I moved in was great. I've always craved the security of my own home. I felt that, despite missing Keith terribly, we were settling.

Keith came over a week later to help with putting carpets down. My mother and father came over as well. They stayed with Laura. Keith stayed for two weeks and I loved having him there but it made it so much harder to stay when he left. I thought I could do it though. He came over three or four times while we were there and each time it got harder to say goodbye. I went back to Ireland a few times to visit him. The love letters and cards kept coming when we returned to Derby. I continued to miss him terribly.

I had my maintenance from Tony going into a bank account in Bray so I would have spending money. I put my father's name as a co-signatory on my account in case I needed money taken out or if there was an emergency – another of my bizarre decisions. One of my visits was for my niece's Communion. Keith said he'd get us a B&B so we could spend time together. When I got to Bray I went to the bank to get some money only to discover it was gone. My father had taken it and not said anything. I was so embarrassed in the bank when they showed me his signature. Angry too. I went to my parents' house and asked him about it. He didn't deny it. Just said they had bills to pay. I took his name off the account and went back to England. I was all loved up after seeing Keith. I started to believe again that we had a future together.

A few weeks later I was back in Bray and I went to the bank to get money only to find my father had been in again and taken money. I was really annoyed. I told the bank it was their fault this time as he'd been taken off as a signatory to the account, and they needed to replace my money. They said that, if they replaced it, they would have to prosecute my father for theft, so I didn't take it any further.

Keith was in my ear during that visit, telling me I should

come back home, that we could make a go of things. Well, I didn't need asking twice. I really wanted us to be together. I went back to England to sell my stuff. My mother and father said they would put me up when I came back until I got sorted with accommodation.

I was coming back home, going to live happily ever after with Keith. It took just a week for me to pack up and sell what I had. I got a van, put the kids and our clothes and a few possessions in it and began the trip back.

It took three hours to drive to the ferry and an hour and a half on it. It was late at night when the boat docked in Dun Laoghaire. The kids were dead tired by then and I was frazzled. My heart leaped when I saw Keith waiting there for us. He hopped into the van and straight away started to moan about how long he'd been waiting for us. I could have screamed. We'd just been through a long, unpleasant boat journey. I knew then I had made a mistake. Again. A bloody big one. How thick could I be? But I had made my bed and now I needed to get on with it.

The children and I went to stay in my mother and father's house. I got myself a job. I went back to driving, delivering pizza, and paid my parents for our board. I went to the council to talk about a house but they told me that, after giving up my home, I'd have to wait a long time to be rehoused. I berated myself for giving the house up in the first place to take off, and then giving up a good house there to come back. God, I was a disaster. I got the kids back into school and kept seeing Keith if only to moan about how hard it was to live back in my parents' house. They'd be OK once I was handing up the money but they talked about me behind my back. I know, I heard it from the others. Strange really, the abuse didn't come into my head; it was locked away, back in the box I kept it in for so much of my life. My mother was her usual self. She did her best to put a wedge between Kelly and me, and Kelly and Kristel. I did my best to please her, handing up money for our keep, so much so that I was weeks ahead in payment. She used most of it to feed the slot machines on Bray seafront. It was another very stressful time in my life.

The kids and I did our best to stay out of the way, but one morning they were getting their breakfast and I heard Kelly go into my parents' bedroom. She was giving out about Kristel leaving the grill on, on the cooker. My mother and father started shouting and giving out. Poor Kristel came in to me, crying, saying she just forgot to turn it off. My mother was shouting at my father to get up and hit her. I jumped out of bed, got dressed and went out to find my father on the landing, looking for Kristel so he could hit her. I told him to calm down, that she hadn't done it on purpose, it was just an accident, but he still wanted to hit her. I started to lose my temper then. My mother was still shouting at him, telling him to find her and beat her. I stood in front of him, telling him that he would not put a hand on her. No way. After more shouting from the two of them, they told me to get my kids and get out. I packed some stuff and left.

We walked out with just the clothes on our backs. I had no money, I had given it all to them. I put the four kids in the car and drove to the council offices. They wanted to put us in a hostel in Dublin for a few nights but I refused because I was worried about junkies in there with my kids so I drove to Des and Alice's house in Greystones. I always could turn to them. They took us in. We stayed with them for a week.

I hounded the council. Nearly two weeks later a house came up in Kilbride Grove in Fassaroe in Bray. I was over the moon. My luck was changing. My own house again! The housing officer from Wicklow County Council met me to look it over. The house had been left in a state and needed a lot of work done to it but I didn't care. The back bedroom windows had Perspex in them instead of glass. I wondered about that but I was so desperate to have our own home again that I let it go. It was a corner house with a side entrance. There were eight-foot walls around the house. There were two bungalows alongside it. One housed an old couple, the other a Traveller family.

Keith was still lurking in the background. I hadn't seen much of him, he wasn't allowed near my mother and father's house. No more had been said, from the time I came home, about us moving in together. What a fool I'd been to believe him. Before moving into the new house I had to go back to my parents for the rest of our things. I knocked on the door and asked for it. They had it packed in black bin bags and left in the hall. My mother said she'd heard I got a house. I said yes, I had, and she replied, 'We did you a favour then.' And she really believed that. She never said anything about the money they owed me.

We settled into our new home in Kilbride Grove. I liked it. I had a flair for decorating and slowly but surely made progress, getting the house sorted. I went to work in a hotel.

I enjoyed the job and got on great with the owners. I progressed from being a waitress to managing the place.

I got great satisfaction from it, I felt like I was doing something worthwhile. The money was better too, which made things easier financially for the first time in my life. I can't remember how or why it was that I started talking to my mother and father again but I did. I felt I had to, to see Kelly.

My kids went back to the local school. Kristel came home one day and told me that the school was doing the Stay Safe Programme and she needed my signature for permission to take part. She had done the programme before but she had repeated a year when we'd returned from Derby. I was so conscious of my children's safety that I was happy for her to do it again. I decided to visit the school a second time to remind them about my past, to remind them to keep an eye on Kelly. The principal was the same but it was a different class teacher. They listened politely to what I had to say but didn't comment. They probably thought I was nuts or wondered why, if that was the case, they hadn't been notified by the gardaí or social services.

Kristel did the programme. I had some chats with her about it, making sure she knew she could come to me if anyone touched her inappropriately or did anything to make her feel uncomfortable.

By now I had told Kristel that Kelly was her sister. I explained that her nanny, my mother, didn't want people to know but that, as long as Kristel was kind to her sister, one day it would work out.

I was still getting the house sorted, doing different

projects as I got the money together. After a short while my father offered to help with decorating. I convinced myself that he was trying, kind of, to say sorry; I made myself believe that, that I had normal parents. Deep down though I knew he was doing it for the money. I gave him what I could and he took it. Some days I couldn't stand having him in the house; I would make excuses why he couldn't come. Other days I'd be fine, I'd talk myself into believing everything was OK.

With all that going on I discovered I was pregnant. At first I was excited. I told Keith. He didn't seem too happy. He'd never even offered to help with the house even though he was earning good money. And he still hadn't spoken about moving in with me. In fact things were just the same: I'd pick him up from the pub at ten o'clock at night and he'd leave early the next morning. It was one of those nights that I told him. He was angry, told me to drop him home to his mother's house. I was crying, worrying about how I would cope, but he just got angrier. When I drove him to his mother's house he jumped out of the car and shouted at me that maybe the baby wasn't his, that I was a whore. I hadn't been with anyone else. It triggered flashbacks of my mother and the kind of things she would say to me. A blind rage descended on me. I revved up the car and went after him, went straight for him, pinning him up against the wall. I realized what I'd done and jumped out, saying I was sorry. He punched me and called me names. I jumped back into the car, in pieces. What the hell was I going to do?

Apart from some abusive texts I didn't hear from Keith over the next few weeks. I was nearly six weeks pregnant and feeling very sick. After a lot of thinking I knew I couldn't go through with the pregnancy. I couldn't put the kids through any of it. I needed to keep working and Keith wasn't going to help me.

I made enquiries, got prices about going to England for an abortion. I don't want to do it, God knows, but what choice do I have? It's hard enough caring and having to provide for the other four on my own. I booked it after going to my friend, crying. She lent me the money to have my pregnancy terminated. It sounds so cold. So clinical. It's booked now. A clinic in London. In three weeks' time I am getting rid of my baby. I am in complete despair. Other than the nasty texts I haven't heard from Keith. I feel completely and utterly alone. I feel overwhelmed a lot of the time. Why did this have to happen when I was getting on well in work and the kids were settled again? Why can't I have some control over my life instead of letting things happen to me? Well, I am taking control now, with this decision. But it's tearing me apart.

Keith was still texting me. One night he asked if he could come up to the house to see me and I went and picked him up. When we got back I told him about my planned trip to England. He didn't believe me so I showed him the tickets for the flight. He didn't offer any help. He just turned and walked out. I really didn't want to do it but I was resigned to it at that stage. I absolutely couldn't raise another child on my own. I was so scared and I cried so much.

The night before I was due to travel to England Keith's former wife, Margaret,[5] rang me and asked if she could come to see me. I agreed. Keith had told her about my plans. I was feeling sick when she arrived.

We went and sat in my bedroom for some privacy. I was

_____
5 Not her real name.

hiding everything from the kids. She told me that she just wanted to see if I was OK. She understood what I was going through. She knew Keith would be no help. We talked for hours, mostly about Keith. She was able to tell me the names he would call me. She made me realize that it wasn't my fault, this bad relationship. Her kindness shocked me. We talked until midnight. The phone went and it was Keith. He wanted to talk if I could go and pick him up.

I said no, it was only a thirty-minute walk, and why wait until after the pub to ring? He called me more names and hung up. Margaret tried her best to console me. I was in bits.

I left for the airport early the next morning. My friend drove me. I cried all the way. I half hoped Keith would be at the airport to stop me but he wasn't. I went ahead and aborted my baby. It took two days to go over and back, two lonely, lonely days. I flew home and when I got to my house, Sharon, the girl that minded my kids while I was gone, told me that Keith had been ringing. About an hour later he rang and screamed 'murdering bitch' down the phone. He did that for about two days.

It was the end of me and Keith as far as I was concerned. I could not continue being around someone so callous and uncaring. It was destroying me and wasn't good for my kids. I had to go back to work and get on with things. I had to hide how I was feeling, to bury what I had done.

10. Driven out of My Home

It was September 1997. Kristel was eleven, Paddy nearly nine, Lewis seven and Deasún just turned two. Six weeks after moving into the house in Kilbride Grove the Travellers next door attacked Kristel. I'd had problems with them since shortly after moving in. They'd been stealing my milk and dumping rubbish in the back garden. Lighted papers were put through my letterbox and paint was daubed on my car. I rang the council a few times but they weren't very quick in getting back to me. The neighbours told me that the house had an awful history, that the Travellers gave terrible abuse to the people living there before me and that the windows had been smashed a few times. It made sense. That was why the windows in the back of the house had been replaced with Perspex by the council. It seems the Travellers were paranoid about being watched and they hated to see anyone at the windows. I just thought, 'To hell with it, I'll keep my head down.'

I had great plans for the house. I was getting on well in the hotel; I'd done a lot of shifts over Christmas when they were busy with parties and I was saving like mad. It helped take my mind off getting rid of the baby. I was still feeling so bad about it, even though, deep down, I knew it was the right decision. I had to be able to work. My kids needed things and the house needed to be done.

The place was really taking shape. I got a new fireplace put in, wooden floors put down. I varnished them myself at night when the kids were asleep. I took to stencilling, did all of the hall and kitchen, anything to keep myself busy and not think of Keith or the baby. My mother and father would call up. Again I let my father do some of the work and paid him for it. I had planned to start on the kitchen next, replacing the old cupboards with new, modern ones.

The months passed. I was still having trouble with the family next door but I tried my best to ignore them. I was in the kitchen one day making lunch. It was July 1998. The kids were sitting around the table at the window, waiting for their food, when we heard stones being thrown at the window. I looked out to see some kids on the wall, shouting in at us. They were the Travellers' children from next door. I closed the blinds and started to put lunch on the table. The next thing the window smashed in on top of us. I grabbed the kids out of the way. They were shocked and frightened. I was shaking. I took them into the sitting room and rang the gardaí and the council. No one from the gardaí came and the council didn't return my calls. 'I'll have to deal with this myself,' I thought.

I decided to go around and try to talk to the parents, find out what the problem was. Maybe no one had tried that before. So I went and knocked on the door. No one answered. Then I heard Kristel scream. She had followed me. Two of the girls had hold of her. They were hitting her.

As I turned to go to her the door opened and a young girl jumped on me. I lost my temper. I needed to get Kristel away. I picked up a sweeping brush that was lying in the garden. 'Come on, come on!' I shouted. 'What have I ever done on you?' The girls let go of Kristel. She ran home. I was enraged. I swung the brush. 'Let's see how you like it,' I thought and I put it through their window. 'Now leave me alone, and don't put your hands on my kids again!' I screamed. I went home, rang the gardaí again and the council.

A garda came up and went around to the Travellers' house. The parents weren't there, only the kids. He told me he got verbal abuse himself from the children. I was really worried at that stage. What would happen when the parents came home? I told the garda I needed help, that I was afraid for our safety. 'What do you want, a babysitter?' he said to me as he turned to leave.

It was late evening. My kids were still upset and were hard to settle. I made them promise me they wouldn't go near the windows. They told me they didn't like the house. Kristel was crying. I told her she'd be fine, she had me; I wouldn't let anything happen to her. I felt such guilt. How could I have gotten into this? Every turn I took was a wrong one. I rang the women's refuge to see if they could help. They told me no, as it wasn't a problem with a partner or husband. They were, however, aware of the Traveller family's history. A lot of good it was, telling me that. It just worried me all the more.

I lit the fire and sat with Kristel after I'd put the boys to bed. She cuddled up beside me and I told her we'd be fine, the doors were locked. A short time later I heard shouting outside and a moment later my sitting-room window was smashed. I grabbed Kristel and ran upstairs to my bedroom. I rang the gardaí from there.

I could hear glass smashing and kicking at my front door.

My bedroom window came in then. I was screaming down the phone for help. I could hear them inside the house now, breaking things downstairs. I was terrified. I put Kristel under my bed and told her to stay there. I could hear them shouting 'Where are you?' I didn't want them getting to the boys. I walked out to the landing and shouted 'I'm here!' and went across to walk down the stairs to them so that they wouldn't come up to my boys' bedroom. Just as I got to the top step they ran up, three young girls, twelve, sixteen and eighteen. They started attacking me. I knew I had to let them do what they wanted, three of them were too many to take on and I didn't want them going after the kids. I didn't know it at the time but Kristel had crawled out from under the bed and across broken glass to get to the phone.

As they punched and kicked me I remember thinking, 'I could push one of them down the stairs.' I could also hear others downstairs, ransacking the place. The girls were tearing at my clothes. One snatched chains from around my neck. I heard neighbours' voices then, above the others – they were trying to get in to help. I got a couple of kicks to the head and couldn't see with the blood in my eyes. Next I heard a man saying 'Get off her!' and a woman's voice. She helped me up. There seemed to be loads of people in my home. The woman was one of my neighbours. I said to her, 'Please get my kids, don't let them see me like this.' 'They're safe, we have them,' she told me. 'What about Kristel?' I asked. 'She's fine too,' I was told. They got a dressing gown for me as my clothes were practically ripped off. Dozens of people were outside when I was brought out of the house. A group of local youths had tried to get into my house to help me. They'd prevented the father of the Traveller family from getting to me. An ambulance was called and the gardaí had arrived by then.

I was taken to hospital but I was worried sick about the kids. I couldn't see out of my eyes they were so badly swollen. I couldn't stop shaking and crying. My friend Angela called to the hospital. I told her I wasn't staying in, my kids would be frantic, I needed to get back to them. She tried to persuade me to stay but I was having none of it. I signed myself out of the hospital. Angela drove me to her house to clean me up and get some clothes for me. She made me a hot drink while I was there. My children had been taken to my sister Christine's house so I went there and stayed with them overnight.

My head is throbbing. I am stiff and sore all over. Here I am again, lying awake, listening to my sleeping children, wondering how in God's name I got us into this mess. Kristel is lying on my arm. I held her until she went asleep. I don't want to move it and wake her. No sleep for me tonight. This is all my fault. If I hadn't met Keith. If I hadn't left the country. If I hadn't come back. Why do I keep doing these things? Always ending up back at square one. First back in Oldcourt on my mother and father's doorstep. Now this. My poor kids. What am I doing to them? This can't go on.

The next morning, early, I went over to my mother's house for a coffee. Christine's is only a few doors away. People were ringing to see if I was OK. I could still hardly see out of my swollen eyes and my head still hurt. A local Fianna Fáil councillor, David Grant, got in touch to tell me there was an emergency meeting in the council offices that day with the residents of the estate and the gardaí. Would I go? I said yes, I would. He said he'd come and collect me.

I borrowed some clothes from Christine and checked on the kids. I cried when I saw Kristel's hands, cut from the glass she'd crawled on. My poor little girl. I had failed to protect them. When it all boiled down to it I couldn't protect my children. I felt awful. I took them to Des and Alice's house. They were the only people I could turn to. I asked them to look after the children for the day for me as I went off to sort out what I would do.

I'm on my way back from Des and Alice's. Kristel was still upset when I left her even though she usually loves going to their house. They've had such a fright. I'm heading back to Christine's to wait for the lift from Councillor Grant to the meeting. A thought comes into my head. What if I don't go? What if I just go away? On my own. Away from everyone. Leave my kids. Just don't go back for them. I mean, look at me. No house, no clothes even. I keep making bad decisions that are hurting them. It's not fair on them. I feel like I've hit rock bottom. I don't know if I have the strength to try all over again to get a home together for us. Is this punishment for me having the abortion? All I feel is despair. Black despair.

No one knows that, I've never admitted it before, that I considered not going back for them that day. I honestly thought they might be better off without me. But I did go back. I got the strength from somewhere to keep going. First I went to the council meeting. A lot of residents were there. The housing officer from the council and the gardaí were there too. As people spoke, all telling different stories of trouble with the family, I realized it wasn't just me. Each and every family on the estate had problems with them. It had been going on for over twenty years. The previous tenants of the house I'd been in left because of them. The council knew this. How could they put me there? A woman on her own with four children?

I'd been told previously that if I left the house I'd be held responsible for abandoning it and I wouldn't be rehoused by the council. But there was simply no way I could return there after the attack. I could not endanger my children by taking them back. I turned my anger on the housing officer. I told him I wanted my clothes and the children's, that day. He told me the council couldn't be responsible for my safety if I decided to go back to the house to get my things. In the meantime, he said, they would put us up in a B&B until they found me alternative accommodation. They had apparently had a change of heart over me being considered as having abandoned the house.

Some of the residents offered to go to the house with me to help get our clothes. They would protect me. I left the meeting very angry. I went back to the house to pack. Neighbours stood outside as I was getting things together. The Travellers did come round and shouted to me that if I moved back in I'd leave in a coffin. The gardaí were there, they heard what was said. I looked around the house, seeing all the work I'd done. All of the hard-earned money I'd put into it was lost.

We were put up in an old hotel that was dirty and horrible. It housed refugees and was crowded and noisy. We went with just our clothes. That first night there I talked to the kids, put on a brave face for them, told them I was OK, but inside I was lonely and very, very scared. I had another sleepless night, another night of beating myself up over what I had put my children through.

I rang the housing officer the next day and told him I wasn't staying there a second night. He got annoyed with me but I wasn't having any of it. 'I'll take photos and go to the papers if I have to,' I told him. I asked him if he'd stay there. Finally he agreed to put us up in a B&B around the corner. It was cleaner but we could only stay there for one night. We packed and went around to it. I ran baths and washed the kids, telling them I'd go to the chipper and we'd have a picnic on the beds when I got back with our food. When they were in their pyjamas I ran across the road to the chip shop. As I stood there waiting for our food I felt a kick on the back of my leg. I nearly jumped out of my skin with fright. I turned around in shock and who was there but Keith. I must have looked a sight with my black eyes. He told me he'd heard what had happened and was worried about me and wanted to know if I was all right and how the kids were.

I was just grateful to have an adult to speak to. I invited him over to say hello to them and he came over. He sat with us as we had our chips. I settled them down afterwards. 'You look tired,' Keith said to me. I told him I was, that I hadn't been sleeping well at all. I asked him if he'd stay for a few hours, just sit and let me sleep, that I'd sleep easier if he did. I was lonely. I just wanted to be held. He said no, that he had made plans with mates and was running late. What a stupid idiot I was to even think he would. I told him to get out and not to come near us again. I didn't sleep well that night either. I cried for most of it. I was worried, we had to get out of the B&B the next morning and we had nowhere to go.

David Grant got in touch the following day to say a house had become available in Greystones. I was so happy and grateful that someone was looking out for us. I would be near my Uncle Des and Aunt Alice too. We agreed David would pick me up and take me to view it. I got excited. 'A bit of light at the end of the tunnel,' I thought. We went out to see it that afternoon. There was a nice garden at the front. When he opened the front door though there was a terrible smell, like a dead body, and the dirt, the state of it, I just thought, 'Oh no, I can't do this all over again.' The councillor agreed it was in an awful condition. 'No way, no way, Fiona, will I let you move into this dump,' he said. We left. I cried all the way back to Bray. My bubble was burst. I felt completely dejected. We got a different B&B that night. We ended up there for three days. To top it all I lost my job in the hotel. I hadn't been able to go in with two black eyes. Nor could I have left my kids alone in the B&Bs. I simply couldn't work with the way things were.

Then, out of the blue, I got a call from some people in Oldcourt in Bray saying that there was a family interested in moving to Greystones who were willing to take the house I'd seen and I could have their place in Oldcourt if the council agreed.

Oldcourt. Imagine. Full circle. I was desperate though, so I agreed.

The council approved the move and said they'd have my stuff packed and moved for me. I wasn't allowed back to the house in Kilbride Grove to pack the rest of our things. So back we went to Oldcourt, number 112 Oldcourt Avenue this time. It was done quickly, we were moved in within a couple of days and the kids were able to keep going to school without interruption.

The new neighbours had heard about my ordeal and were good to me; one sent in strawberries and one of the men came to tell me they were there if I needed anything. My first night in that house was hard. Nothing could really replace what I had lost. Not the material things, but the feeling of security that we'd lost, and my ability to protect my children. I felt I had failed them. I had an alarm installed and panic buttons but I still couldn't sleep right. I would lie awake night after night going over my stupid life in my head. How was I getting it so wrong? I loved my kids with all my heart and they were not having the life they deserved. Yet they never complained.

I was still angry with the council for housing me, as a single mother with four children, in the Kilbride Grove house when they knew the history of the family who lived next door. I went to see a solicitor about taking a case against them. He set the wheels in motion.

Keith was back in contact with me, on and off, after that night in the B&B. It was always the same, him wanting to come up after the pub. I have to admit I did let him sometimes. I was so lonely and scared, especially at night. I always felt awful afterwards though and would give out to myself for being so weak.

My friend Angela called over one day to ask me if I'd waitress in a pub in Booterstown. She had started there as a manageress and needed help. I was delighted. I really needed to work to support the children properly and because so much needed doing to the new house we'd been moved to. It was a mess. My father offered to do work for me. I let him. I told myself that it was normal, this was what normal dads did for their daughters.

I'd begin my shift in the restaurant at five in the evening and be home between eleven and twelve o'clock. I loved it. After I'd been there for about a month Angela left and I took over her role. I'd work five to six nights a week. The hours were great because I'd be home all day and was there when the kids came in from school.

With Kristel, who was fourteen by then, in charge the boys would put themselves to bed at seven o'clock. I was strict about that, I'd ring home at least four or five times a shift, checking on them, making sure they were in and settled down. That job made me finally begin to believe I was good at something. I'd organize the staff when we had a tour in, supervise the arrival of the tour group, sort out the wages, the set-up, and I'd take bookings. The bosses were so good to me. They let me make all the calls home I needed and take calls when the children rang me, they never complained. I made good money on tips and I was spending every penny on the children and the house.

Kristel was into line dancing in a big way then. She was taking part in competitions and I needed money for her outfits and for weekends away competing. My boss kindly allowed Kristel's line-dancing club to fundraise in the pub. The line dancers won the All Ireland Championships and were heading to Canada to compete straight after Christmas so I had to raise a lot of money. It was a ten-day trip and she needed the money for flights, her hotel, food and outfits. Without that job I would have been lost. Kristel had asked her dad for help in getting the funds together for the trip to Canada. He agreed to help but when the time came she rang him for the money he'd promised her and he told her he didn't have it. I remember her crying down the phone saying, 'This is not fair on Mammy, she does it all.'

I worked long hours before and over Christmas to try to get all four of them what they wanted. I loved Christmas since I'd had the kids and always vowed theirs would be nothing like the ones I'd had as a child. We'd be all excited in the weeks beforehand. The kids would help me as much as they could. I would draw up a Christmas cleaning roster, things like cleaning the fridge out, cleaning bathrooms, hoovering. They would tick the boxes after they'd done their jobs and knew that because they'd done their bit there'd be an extra-nice present from their mammy on Christmas Eve. It was our tradition. I'd do my shopping in the middle of the night in the 24-hour supermarkets on the way home from work. I remember being so tired. Occasionally the boys would wake and hear me when I got home and they'd come down and carry the shopping in from the car for me, sometimes at two or three in the morning.

I'd get up early on Christmas Eve to prepare the veg, make the stuffing and the trifle before I went to work. The chef at work would cook my turkey and ham for me and I'd finish at about four in the afternoon.

One year when I got home the kids had the table all set and ready for Christmas Day as a surprise. They had also bathed themselves and were in their pyjamas.

*

'Jingle bells, jingle bells, jingle all the . . .' 'WAY!' all four of them shout in unison. I laugh and launch into 'Rudolph the Red-Nosed Reindeer'. They join in. We are in the car, driving back from Dublin. It's the evening of Christmas Eve. I'd taken them to see Arnott's window, as a surprise.

I bundled them into the car, in their pyjamas, when I got home from work and took them first to my Uncle Des and Aunt Alice's house for a quick visit before going into the city centre. I point out houses with loads of Christmas lights on them as we pass now, on the way back home. They are tired out and ready for bed. We talk about which houses are the best decorated. They are happy, excited. Kristel looks at me from the passenger seat, a big smile on her face. The boys are in the back, still talking about Arnott's window. They're laughing at what happened to me. There was a cart with a horse parked in the street when we got out of the car. I went to pet the horse and it sneezed all over me. The kids thought it was hilarious. 'What happened to the singing?' I ask now. Kristel starts up, 'You better watch out, you better not cry . . .' and we all join in. It's at times like this that I feel it's all worthwhile. I feel like it's me and my kids against the world.

I was delighted that Kristel got to go to Canada that year. My boss had given me a Christmas bonus and I used that to pay for it.

Keith was still hovering around. I'd seen him with another woman. It hurt and I cried over it, because sometimes the loneliness was so hard. Just to have come home from work and have an adult to talk to would have been nice. He was still playing his games with me. It was as if, as soon as he thought I wasn't interested in him any more, he'd hound me.

My job was a lifesaver. I was good at it. It was one of the

happier times in my life. I do wonder sometimes how my boss put up with me because the demands of my children often impinged on my job in the years that I was there. Like the time, while Kristel was in Canada and I was in the middle of service one night, Paddy rang me to tell me he was packing his bags and moving out. He told me he was going to live with my brother Richard. I was shocked. I couldn't believe it. Why would a twelve-year-old boy want to do such a thing? I told my boss I had to leave, walked out of the restaurant and drove home in a panic. When I got there Paddy was packed and ready to go. I was crying, asking him why he would want to go. It turned out that while I was in work his Uncle Richard would call around and talk to him, telling him he was being abused, that all the cleaning he was being made to do was unfair, that I treated the children like slaves and I was wrong in expecting Paddy to be in off the street and in bed so early. Richard told Paddy he'd give him more freedom and his own bedroom.

I was so upset. I rang Des and Alice and they sent their son to our house. My cousin was like a little brother to me. He got Paddy on his own to talk some sense into him. I just sat in the kitchen, crying, wondering why one of my children would want to leave me. I rang Richard to ask him what he was playing at. He started shouting at me that I was an unfit mother, repeating that I treated my kids like slaves. He said he was going to report me. We got Paddy to change his mind. I was so relieved. I didn't want Paddy living with Richard. He smoked hash all the time, kept his big hash pipe on the kitchen table, in full view. I did not want my son living with that.

I drove to the airport to collect Kristel, still upset with Richard. I didn't want to spoil her homecoming but she could tell I'd been crying. I wouldn't have anything to do with Richard after that.

I did feel sometimes during those years that I wasn't around for my children as much as I would have liked, but I needed to work. The house was getting done, slowly, and starting to look nice.

Around this time rumours started to circulate about me. People couldn't understand how I could have a nice car and afford to have my house done up. There was talk of me driving into Dublin each evening and selling myself for sex. I heard all this from a man who was doing work in my house. He couldn't understand how I was able to pay him upfront and not on a weekly basis like a lot of his clients, so he asked around about me and was told I was a prostitute. He then came around and made me an offer. I threw him out of my home and told him I'd tell his wife. He never came back. How spiteful people were. Some of these people's children had come to the line-dancing fundraising event, and others had come to the pub for dinner, so they knew I was working there, yet they still saw fit to say such things about me.

11. Top of the World to Depths of Despair

I worked in that pub for three years and I loved every minute of it. It was thanks to that job that I got an opportunity to travel. My aunt and uncle minded the kids and I went on my first ever foreign holiday. I got the travel bug then and decided it would be nice for my kids to see some other countries too, do all the things I never got the chance to do. I took them away as much as I could, just me and them. Over time we went to Spain, Tunisia, Malta and Crete. My best friend lived in Malta and I even sent Paddy to stay with her so that he could attend the Gary Neville Soccer School for three months.

It wasn't all plain sailing, those years, especially with three boys. They'd fight like cats and dogs. Trying to keep them in line, keep the house clean, keep on top of the washing as well as working was bloody hard work. Sometimes it would all get on top of me. I went to use the DVD player one day and it wouldn't work. I sat on the floor and cried my eyes out. The kids would catch me at times like that and I'd feel so bad. At other times I could have strangled them.

One night it was snowing heavily and a lot of kids were out playing and having snowball fights. My boys asked if they could go out and I said no. I could hear them crying in their bedroom and felt sorry for being so hard on them so I agreed to let them out for an hour. Paddy came back on his own after the hour. I asked him where Lewis was. He told me he'd been arrested. He was ten. I panicked, rang the gardaí and asked them what had happened and where he was. He'd been throwing snowballs at cars with a group of young fellas and the gardaí were called. When they arrived Lewis was cheeky to them so they took him down to the station. They said they were on their way to my house with him.

By the time the squad car arrived I was like a bull. Lewis didn't even have time to get out of the car, I was out the door in my nightclothes, shouting at him for getting into trouble with the gardaí. It was a big fear for me, that my boys would end up in trouble. I'd even taken them to visit my brother a couple of times when he was in prison, so they could see where they'd end up if they got on the wrong side of the law. I wanted more than that for them. I was overprotective of them, I knew that. I probably went overboard at times.

Kristel was a clever little girl. We were very close. All problems with her would be solved in my bed with a hot-water bottle and a hot chocolate. She was also very perceptive. She'd watch and see more than I realized. One night she was in bed in her room, which was beside mine, and I was sitting up in bed with a cup of coffee. We were chatting back and forth as we'd often do. She was fourteen at the time. I was heading off for a week's holiday the next day and was all packed and ready to go. My cousin was coming to mind the children for the week.

A moment later Kristel came into my room. She looked very worried. 'Mam,' she said, 'I need to ask you something.'

'Yes,' I asked, 'what is it?' We were always honest with one another but I could tell she was holding back.

'It's hard to ask you, Mam,' she said.

'Kristel,' I told her, 'you know you can ask me anything. I will give you an honest answer.'

She'd started to cry. 'I feel awful asking you this, Mam, or even thinking it, but were you abused by Granddad?'

She must have seen the shock on my face because she began sobbing then.

'Yes,' I said. 'Yes, I was.'

'Oh, Mammy,' she said. 'It all makes sense now. Now I understand.'

She got into bed beside me and I cuddled her.

'I am sorry, Mammy, so sorry.'

I was crying now and wishing with all my heart that I wasn't going away the next morning. I didn't want to leave her in that state.

'What makes sense, Kristel?' I asked her.

'Oh you, Mam, you not letting me go on sleepovers, how protective you are.'

I looked at her little face. 'Kristel, I will tell you anything you want to know,' I said.

I explained that maybe the week away would be good; she could think of questions she wanted to ask and I would answer them when I got back. I settled her eventually and she went to sleep beside me. I had to go the next morning, it was all organized, but I was so tormented. All the good had gone out of it for me.

I rang home when I got to the airport and told my cousin what had happened the night before. I asked her to keep a special eye on Kristel while I was away. I worried about her the whole time I was gone, what was going through her mind when I wasn't there. And how was I going to tell her about what had happened to me if she wanted to know? Then I thought of the various bits and pieces I had written over the years when I just couldn't cope with things that were going on in my life. I had done that from early childhood. I had stuff in notebooks and scraps of paper. I came up with the idea of trying to put my scribblings in some sort of order, filling in the gaps in my memories as much as I could, and then letting her read it. I didn't feel I could tell her to her face. It was hard to see her hurt and upset. Such a brave girl and so understanding. I was worried about the effect it would have on her schooling with her exams coming up. What a horrible thing for a young girl to have to carry in her head. It was so unfair.

Random, painful memories. Images and smells. Still I've decided to start writing. My own daughter, Kristel, is fourteen now and my boys are growing up. Someday I want them to know about the kind of childhood I had. If I can't talk to them about what happened to me at least I can show them my writings and they'll understand why I am the way I am. Overprotective of them. Constantly stressing to them to be careful in toilets and changing rooms. Not wanting them to go on sleepovers. Warning them over and over to tell me if anyone touches them inappropriately.

I felt at this stage that I was needed at home more. I'd started managing the cloakroom in a nightclub at weekends as a favour for a friend so, when the chance came, I decided to take that job on permanently. I handed in my notice at the pub. The nightclub hours were from eleven in the evening until four in the morning. It meant I was around in the evenings during the week, and at weekends the kids would be in bed before I left. I also went back to doing deliveries for a Chinese restaurant on Tuesday evenings to keep up my level of income. Lewis would come with me on those; he'd run up to the doors with the food as I turned the car around, take the money and give change. I'd let him keep the tips so he earned a bit of pocket money. With his help I was fast and it meant we got to spend time together.

I was pleased with this new working arrangement. The nightclub was great, it was like getting paid to socialize. I didn't drink at that time but I loved the music. Kristel would come with me some nights. She loved doing this, loved having me to herself for a while.

I was still getting the house sorted. My dad was doing wallpapering and tiling for me. I'd just get out of his way, leave him to it. I still chose not to see it for what it was: a way of getting money out of me. I paid for my parents to go to Malta for a week with Kelly. I was so desperate to have a good family and I wanted Kelly to have holidays too. Nothing I did was ever good enough though. I'd still hear horrible stories about myself, mostly started by them.

I began to take courses at weekends. I paid for them myself. I trained as a nail technician so I could do nails from home as a hobby and to make some extra money. At one stage I had a number of regular customers. Another course I took was training to become a respite worker with the elderly. I got a job doing night shifts at a nursing home but it only lasted about eight months. Of all the jobs I had, that one was the hardest, but it was also the most rewarding. The trouble was that I would get too attached to the residents and would want to spend time with them, sit with them. It was physically exhausting too. I'd drive home from my shift early in the morning and couldn't walk from the car into the house my feet would be so sore. I'd have about fifteen patients to care for and would have to carry their breakfasts, tray by tray, up two flights of stairs. I packed that job in as I really wasn't able to cope with it.

I got a court date for my case against the council over the house they'd put me in where I'd been attacked. It was heard in the Circuit Court in March 2002. The courthouse was in Wicklow town. My friend drove down with me for company. Apart from the family court hearing when Tony sought custody of Lewis, this was the first time ever I was to be involved in a court case and I was pretty nervous. As I stood outside waiting to go in I remember thinking to myself that there were a lot of council officials there and just me on my side. 'How in God's name will I win this?' I thought. My friend sat with me in the courtroom and ran for coffee to keep me calm. When the case was called I had to take the witness stand, swear on the Bible and give my version of things.

The council officials really tried to defend themselves, more or less saying I'd been an awkward tenant, moving around a lot, and that I'd required the house as a matter of urgency for myself and the children and it was the only one available. My barrister made a good case though, arguing that I had been exposed to an unusual danger in being housed there. The court heard about the previous tenants, who had left because of the actions of the Traveller family. Judge Raymond Groarke ruled in my favour and awarded me €6,826. He spoke about the 'appalling situation' I'd had to put up with and said there had been a failure on the part of the council to comply with my rights in providing me with a house that was fit and habitable.

When he made his ruling I was aware of a lot of people running in and out. Until then, I hadn't realized the full extent of the case and the importance of it. Outside the court reporters gathered around me, telling me that this was a landmark case, it was setting a precedent because never before had someone held the council responsible for the actions of their tenants. I got calls from radio stations and newspapers looking for my story. I felt proud of myself. I had stood up for myself and decided that people in authority wouldn't treat me like dirt. It felt good.

That weekend my kids nominated me as Mother of the Year in a competition on the local radio station and I won. People from the radio station arrived at my door with flowers, chocolates and concert tickets. What a surprise it was. I was so proud of my kids. The radio station interviewed me and Kristel at the house, asking her about me. It made it all so worth it. I used the money awarded by the court to get gas heating into the house, something I'd always wanted.

With my family you wouldn't be on a high very long. I was working in the nightclub one Friday when my phone rang. It was my older brother, Austin. He was crying down the phone. It was a shock to hear his voice. I hadn't heard from him for such a long time. 'Fiona, I've done something awful, I really have,' he told me. I don't know why but I just knew what he was going to say. I could feel my body stiffen.

'Please don't tell me, Austin, please don't tell me you have interfered with a child.'

'Yes,' he said. 'Yes, I did and I need to get out of here, I'm heading for the boat and will be home tomorrow.'

I didn't know what to say. I heard myself telling him, 'You are not coming to me, I can't have you stay in my home. I will see you tomorrow and talk then.'

All sorts went through my mind. *Why me? Why phone and tell me of all people?*

I thought back to my early years in England. There had been talk before about Austin interfering with family members. I don't know many of the details as I was having my own problems at the time, trying to stop my father from being at me.

I got home from work around four in the morning. Kristel was with me and on the way home I told her about Austin and warned her never to have anything to do with him and that he was never to be in our house.

Kristel is in bed. I've looked in on the others. They are fast asleep. I'm sitting at the kitchen table with a cup of coffee. Not much point in me going to bed, I know I won't sleep. I feel a headache starting behind my eyes. Thoughts are churning around in my brain. I keep replaying Austin's call in my head, what he said, what I said. God, it's just too much. I can't bear it. Can't bear to think about what he has done.

Early the next morning I rang Richard and told him about the call from Austin. Richard said he'd drive to Rosslare to meet him. While he was doing that I told Christine that Austin was coming. We were all gathered in Richard's house when Austin and Richard arrived back. Austin was in tears as he explained that he had been kicked out by his partner because she found out he had interfered with her young daughter.

Richard said he'd tell our parents. Austin said no, he didn't want them to know. When he was asked why he said, 'Because I got this off him.'

I was taken aback to hear him say that and I could see the others were too. I asked him why he said that, what he meant by it.

'Because I would hide in the wardrobe and watch Daddy with you,' he said.

I was astonished. I couldn't believe that he had come out with this. On occasions my father had raped me upstairs in the bedroom he shared with my mother. He'd do that during afternoons when my mother was out and he thought there was no one else in the house. There were built-in wardrobes in that room, the only wardrobes in the house.

I was upset for two reasons. First, mortified that he'd actually seen me being abused. And second, angry that he hadn't spoken up for me in all the years I'd been called a liar. I asked Christine if she'd heard what he said. She nodded.

Richard then said that he also used to hide in the wardrobe and watch. Oh God, this was just too much. I could feel the anger well up inside me, outstripping my embarrassment.

'Why are you only telling me this now, after all these years? And you, Richard, disowned me,' I said. 'Why aren't you getting Mam and Dad down to explain themselves?'

Austin refused. I told him I would help him all I could if

he got help to stop wanting to abuse children but that I wouldn't help him hide what he'd done. He was not to come to my home or be anywhere near my daughter.

I left the house in a temper and when I got outside I rang the gardaí and told them about Austin arriving in the country, and that he had abused a child in England. The garda asked if the child's mother had made a complaint. I said no and was told there was nothing they could do. I was distraught.

I went to my parents' house in a rage. My father was sitting by the fire, as always, and my mother was in the kitchen. I told her Austin had come back and that he didn't want to see them. I told her what he had done but there was no reaction. No disgust, shock or horror. She just said, 'Yeah, but why doesn't he want to speak to us?'

I started shouting at her. 'Do you realize that he reckons he got this off Dad?'

'That's not my fault,' she said.

My father walked in then and she started to tell him. I turned on my heels and walked out. I went home to bed. I was in tears. What to do? I couldn't just do nothing. I was so down. *This dirt in my family is spreading and no one is listening or helping.*

I was also trying to deal with the fact that Austin and Richard had known I was telling the truth all along.

The following day I went down to Richard's house. He and Austin had chatted all night. Austin had more or less convinced Richard that the child he abused had been flirting with him and that it was all her fault. Disgraceful. I could see the big cover-up starting to happen. I got Austin on his own and told him about confronting Mam and Dad the evening before. I also asked him about the stories I'd heard that he'd done it before, and he admitted they were true. Again I told him he had better not come anywhere near my house or daughter. I stayed away from them for a few days after that; I needed to sort out my head.

I went down to Richard's a few days later and my mother and father were sitting there, all of them chatting casually. I was shocked. Apparently Austin had decided he wanted to talk to them. I don't know what was said but it was like none of it had happened. I had to leave. I felt like I really was beating my head against a brick wall. How could people be so stupid? I was furious.

Later, when I guessed my mother and father would have left his house, I went back to Richard's. Austin was in the sitting room. 'Why are you all trying to hide what is going on in our family? Why are you doing this, hiding the dirt?' I asked him. I told Richard he couldn't have Austin staying in his house. Richard got angry with me, told me to shut up, but I refused, I told him it was wrong.

Richard snapped and went for me, grabbed me by the neck with both hands around my throat and pinned me against the wall. Austin jumped up and made him let me go. I fell to the floor. Richard went into the kitchen saying he was getting a knife. Austin helped me up and led me out the front door. He put his back to it. Richard came into the hall but Austin refused to let him out the door to get me. My neck was badly marked. I ended up at the doctor's. That was it for me. I felt I just couldn't do it any more. I decided to have no more to do with Richard.

A week or two later I heard from Austin's ex-wife who told me his daughter wanted to come and stay with her dad. I told her why Austin had come home and said I would be worried if her daughter came. We agreed she would come but that she would stay in my house. She wouldn't be alone with her father, and I could keep an eye on her.

Austin was in my mother's house when I next saw him. I told him his daughter was coming over to see him but would be staying in my house. He didn't take that well. 'Are you saying I'd hurt my daughter? Who do you think you are? You have no right to get involved,' he shouted at me.

My mother piped up to say, 'Sure she can stay here.'

I decided there was no point in arguing with them so I left and rang Austin's ex-wife and told her not to let her daughter come, that I couldn't guarantee her protection. We agreed she wouldn't come to visit after all.

This evil disease in my family was spreading and I couldn't stop it. I told Austin if what he did was covered up I wouldn't have anything to do with him. I never spoke to Austin again after that.

12. A Death in the Family

A few months later I heard that Austin, Richard and his family were moving back to England. I was surprised at the news. Richard was giving up his council house. I didn't see him before he went and never got to say goodbye to his children.

I had tried talking to Christine about what Austin and Richard had said in front of her – that they had both watched our father rape me – but she brushed me off and made it clear that she wasn't going to talk about it any further.

I felt myself getting depressed after that. My need to see Kelly made me decide to bury things again but it was tough. I'd spend a few days away from my parents and then I'd pop in when I felt strong enough to handle things. I found it hard putting on a smile for my kids and my job, but I would force myself.

Some months after my brothers had gone back to England Richard phoned to say that Austin had abused another little girl. I couldn't speak I was so upset. How could they let this happen?

The police were involved this time but Austin didn't know at first; he was away for the weekend. They were planning to arrest him when he got back. Two days later I was out doing deliveries for the Chinese restaurant with Lewis when I got a call from my father. Austin had been found dead earlier that day. He'd put a pipe from the exhaust into his car and gassed himself. I felt weak. I was sitting in the car, waiting for Lewis to come back from a house he was delivering food to. I felt my chest tighten, as if I couldn't breathe. I could scarcely take it in. My big brother was dead. My big brother. Dead.

I went back to work and told them I had to finish early. I drove home and then I fell apart. I was up all night crying. I kept thinking of us as kids, how Austin had tried to mind me, protect me. How had it come to this?

Was he scared the police were after him? Or did he do it to stop himself from hurting little girls? I believe that's why he took his own life. He had shown remorse; I'd seen it that night he came home, he felt bad for abusing his partner's daughter.

At that time I had been seeing a guy, Larry.[6] I had met him on a night out with my Aunt Alice. We were dancing in a late-night bar in Bray and he had asked me for my phone number and said he wanted to take me out for a meal. He rang me the next day and we chatted. He asked me out for dinner two days later and I went. I began seeing him regularly after that. He would bring me flowers. I told him everything about my past.

I fell for Larry in a big way. And, stupid as I was, yet again I didn't read the signs, particularly his disappearing acts. I would ask him questions and he would convince me I was imagining things that weren't there. I would drive up to his house late at night after work and he wouldn't be home and

6 Not his real name.

when I mentioned it to him the next day he would call me a liar. There were times when I felt as if I were going mad.

When I told him about my brother he came down to spend the night with me yet he couldn't hold me or put his arms around me.

'Why would you cry after what he did?' he asked.

'I know,' I said. 'But I can't help it.'

I went downstairs to my sitting room. I was there, crying, when I heard Kristel move about upstairs. She went into my bedroom and shouted at Larry, saying, 'Don't you care? My mother is breaking her heart crying, can't you even console her? Why don't you just get out?'

She came downstairs to me and put her arms around me. Why was I falling to bits after what Austin did? I don't know, but I was. He was still my brother. The one of my brothers and sisters I'd been closest to.

I heard the front door slam. Larry had got up and walked out. I was on my own again. There was no one to share the pain with.

My poor kids had to carry all this on their shoulders. Des and Alice phoned to see if I was OK. So did other aunts and uncles on my mother's side. I said I was fine. I wasn't their problem. No point in worrying them.

My mother and father travelled to Derby to identify Austin's body. They were gone for about three days. They organized the funeral while they were there with the help of Laura and Richard. When they came back they told me the funeral would be a week later. I still wasn't sure if I was going to go. How could I? He had abused young girls. Yet he was my brother. I was so mixed up.

I went to talk to some of my aunts and uncles, including Des and Alice. I was feeling guilty for wanting to go. I couldn't understand my feelings. Des and Alice offered to mind the kids for me if I wanted to go. They even helped me with money. I had some but they didn't think it was enough.

My mother and father were doing my head in when they came back from England, going on about how hard it was on them, all the travelling, the expense. They'd tried to get reimbursed for the cost of their tickets and were complaining about how little the social welfare and the St Vincent de Paul helped. It was all 'pity me'. Nothing about their dead son or why he had killed himself.

So the hardest thing about deciding if I would go to the funeral was wondering if I could travel in their company and keep my mouth shut. I was sick of listening to them. Not a tear shed and yet I believed Austin ended up in the state he did, and doing what he did, because of them. It was their fault.

In the end I decided that saying goodbye to my brother was more important than my feelings about my parents. I would just have to control and hide my emotions and travel over to say goodbye. I needed to go. I would just go and say goodbye to the little boy, the brother who had tried to protect me, the brother who would walk to the shops on dark nights with me, who would do the dishes with me when we were dragged out of bed in the middle of the night. I hated what he did to those girls but wasn't killing himself his way of saying sorry for what he had done?

We were all going – my parents, Christine, me, Kelly.

Kelly was another reason I wanted to go. We travelled over by ferry and train. I was staying with an uncle when I got there. I was glad to get away from my mother and father. I knew I'd snap if I stayed in their company. We arrived at Laura's the day before the funeral. Christine and I offered to get and prepare food for after the funeral. I was glad to have something to do – it was my way of contributing and keeping busy.

I was quite nervous about going to the funeral home. As I went to walk into the room where Austin's body was laid out the first thing I noticed was a strange smell. Then I saw the coffin over in a corner, against the wall. The reality of it hit me in the face like a slap. I cried out 'Ah no!' and just stood there, unable to move. I told myself to cop on. I walked over slowly to the coffin. Austin's head was resting on a pillow. I half expected him to sit up and go 'Ha ha!' to me. Closer now I noticed the smell again, a burning smell, like cinders in a fire. I could see all the black in his nails and I realized the smell had to do with the way he'd killed himself, the fumes from the exhaust pipe. I stood beside him, looking at him, thinking, 'He is so handsome, tall and dark. What a waste.'

Then it came into my mind, the reason why he killed himself. I had to shake myself back to reality. I could hear Christine sobbing behind me. I touched Austin's hand. It was cold and hard. He was in a nice grey suit. I started to talk to him in my head. I said to him, 'I know you are sorry for what you did. I know you did what you had to do to stop yourself. Thank you for that. But I will miss you.'

Anger started to bubble up inside me then. I had to leave.

I couldn't cope with all the feelings. I went outside and waited for the others to come out.

We left the funeral home and went back to Laura's house. I got stuck in with preparing the food for the next day. We were there doing the food until late and I hadn't heard from my uncle. I needed him to come and collect me and take me to his house. He wasn't answering his phone. It was looking like I had nowhere to stay. I felt lost and so alone. Much to my dismay I ended up having to stay in the same house as my parents. Their friend was a lovely woman but my mother spent the evening giving out to her about everything to do with the arrangements. I went to bed and left them talking.

I've just woken. In those few seconds between sleep and wakefulness I forget where I am and why I am here. Then realization dawns. This is the day I say my last goodbye to my brother. I fell asleep last night thinking about the times we'd stuck together when we were young. How close we were. I think about the unhappy life Austin had. His childhood was miserable. One of cruelty and deprivation. I remember the night I saw him sleeping in the field in front of the house after he was put out by my mother. I am overcome with sadness.

Not only did he have to carry the demons of his unhappy childhood into his adult life, he carried a much darker legacy. He turned into an abuser, like my father. That destroyed him.

I got up with a heavy heart, put on my black suit and headed back to the funeral home. I stopped to get flowers on the way. I got a rose from me, and four more, one from each of my children. I spoke to Austin again in my mind as I laid the flowers in the coffin with him. 'Austin, these are from me and the kids to let you know we love you and that we know you are sorry.' I could see a spliff in his pocket; I guessed Richard had been down and put it there. It annoyed me. 'Do you have to make a show of us all the time?' I thought. I kissed Austin and said goodbye to him for the last time.

The funeral left from Laura's house. I was with my parents, Christine, Laura and Kelly. We drove behind the coffin for about forty-five minutes. All along the way I just kept looking at the hearse in front. I kept thinking, 'In that coffin is my brother's body and it's their fault.' I stared at my mother and father. Their fault. When we arrived at the crematorium there were a few people there that I didn't know. I presume they were friends of Austin. His ex-wife and daughter were there too. As we walked in I grabbed his daughter's hand and took her with me. It was only fair that she stood with the family.

The service was lovely but the music made me cry. Songs from a CD of Phil Collins's *Urban Renewal* were played. That CD had been playing in the car when Austin took his life.

Then the curtains closed and he was gone. It was the last I would see of my big brother.

I looked at my mother. Not a tear. 'Why can't you cry?' I thought.

Outside, after the ceremony, I just stood there weeping. I felt all alone, set apart from everyone. Austin's ex-wife came over and hugged me. We headed back to the pub near Laura's, where the food was laid out. Austin's partner and her family were there and all his friends came back.

When one of my uncles decided to leave the reception to collect his camper van at Laura's before driving home, I decided to head back with him. As we walked he asked what was going on. He sensed that something wasn't right.

'Don't you know?' I asked. 'Don't you know what he did, why he killed himself?'

He didn't. I told him all about it. He was shocked. I don't know if he believed me. I guess it must have been hard to believe. None of us saying a word. A big cover-up.

The next day I went into town. I didn't want to be near anyone. I sat in a coffee shop for a while. We were all heading home that evening and I couldn't wait. Afterwards, as I walked around the town, I bumped into my mother and father. They'd been shopping. They had to buy new suitcases to carry home all they'd bought.

Larry came to pick me up at the ferry port and drive me home. I asked him to stop at a shop for milk on the way. When I went into the shop I got the shock of my life. Larry's picture was on the front of a newspaper in connection with his sex life. All consenting adults involved but it was nothing I had known about or wanted to know about. I said nothing on the way to my house but when we got there I told him to get the hell out, that I wasn't going to be dragged into his shit.

Two days later I got a phone call from Richard in England. He had all kinds of grievances about the funeral and who had paid for what. Because of this he said he wasn't sending Austin's ashes home; he was giving them to Austin's ex-partner instead. I asked him to let us have them, to bury them, so that we would have somewhere to visit. But he wouldn't change his mind.

We had a Mass organized for a few days later. As we had no ashes for it I got a photo of Austin blown up. It was all we had.

What Austin had done was never spoken about again. His photograph was hung in my parents' hall and they spoke about him as if he were a god. I didn't know if Kelly knew about Austin. My mother made a great job of hiding the true story and getting people to believe her version.

Things were never the same in the family after Austin's death; divisions became deeper and more bitter. Everyone was angry with everyone else.

13. Driven to the Edge of Destruction

Even though I had ended things with Larry the night he'd met me from the ferry after Austin's funeral, I was still seeing him on and off. I knew he was no good for me but I felt fat and worthless. I told myself Larry part-time was better than nothing. Sure, who else would want me?

The kids could see what he was doing to me. They started to hate him and wanted him to stay away from me. They begged me to get rid of him. I would for a few weeks but he would make silent phone calls all the time, never letting me forget he was around. He would drive up and down outside my house at night. I would be feeling low and lonely and he would ring and I would be right back where I started. This went on for quite a while and the anger would bubble away inside me. I was still going to my mam and dad's sometimes to see Kelly, still trying to pretend all was normal.

It was around Kristel's eighteenth birthday when things came to a head. I hadn't spoken to him in weeks and was planning a party in the house when he rang to say he had a present for her. He also had a present for me, he said. It had been my birthday seven weeks before. I let him call to the house with the gifts. He started to tell me how much he missed me and, of course, I caved in as I had done so many times before. He said he would be down that night for the party and I agreed to let him come.

The party went ahead with no sign of him; I had some drink, which I don't normally take, and started to feel such a fool, letting him play with my head. What a bloody idiot I was.

Late that night, after the party, I got into my car and drove to his place to confront him. I wanted to find out what he had gained from treating me like that. I banged on his front door. I could hear a woman shouting at him to get the keys to open the door but he wouldn't. I shoved the necklace he'd given me through the letterbox, yelled at her to tell him to leave me alone, and went back home feeling stupid. What more did I deserve?

The next day I got phone calls from Larry, telling me the woman I'd heard in his house was his ex-wife, that she'd taken over the house and he hadn't even been there. God, he was so convincing. Later I rang his house phone and she answered. First, she started to say she was his wife, that they were back together. He had told her I was stalking him and wouldn't leave him alone. When I told her how long I'd been seeing him she changed her story and told me she'd been seeing him for over a year and wasn't his ex-wife; that he'd told her to say that.

After we'd talked for about an hour, exchanging stories about Christmas and the dates he disappeared, it all started to make sense. He had played me for such a fool.

She then started to tell me the story he'd told her about me and about my past, that my father had abused me, how crazy and screwed up I was because of it. There was worse to come. She said he told her I'd given my father my own daughter to abuse. I was horrified. That cut deep. I was in bits, I couldn't say any more so I hung up.

All day those words spun around in my head. That night

I went to work. I couldn't stop thinking of what had been said to me on the phone. He had taken my honesty and openness and twisted it into something terrible. I was sickened and devastated.

I got home from work at about three in the morning. I couldn't sleep. Everything was still churning around in my brain. I felt I had to make him pay. I got into my car, drove up to his place and parked nearby. It was pitch dark. Normally I'm afraid of the dark but not this night. I was so full of anger and rage; filled with an overwhelming need to get him back. I climbed over a gate and went into a storage shed where I knew he kept a lot of materials for his work. I took out a lighter and found something to set alight.

I walked calmly to my car and drove home. I'll never forget the feeling I had, the feeling of revenge and how good it felt. Finally I had done something to stand up to him.

About half an hour later, as I lay in bed, I heard the noise of the fire engines racing up the road. I sat up and smiled to myself. 'That'll be the last time you'll mess with me, Larry,' I thought. I lay down again and went to sleep.

The following day I got a phone call from Larry's girl-friend, asking me if I had been at his place the night before, saying that someone had set fire to the shed. I was dying to say yes, dying to gloat, but I knew it was a trick, they were probably recording the phone call. So, much as I would have liked to let them know what I'd done, I said no and acted the innocent.

I'd been thinking that revenge really is sweet, like they say. And it was for a while. Now though the reality of what I did has sunk in. Oh

God. This really is serious. What was I thinking? This has to stop. I could lose my kids, behaving like this. Letting my anger get the better of me. I've caused probably thousands of euros' worth of damage. I've committed arson! If I don't calm down I'll ruin my children's lives. God knows things are hard enough for them already. Nothing is worth that. I need to change. No more men in my life until I do something about me.

I'd stand in front of the mirror and look at myself. Fat and ugly. I had got into the habit of comfort eating and my weight had ballooned. I was full of self-loathing. No wonder I attract scumbags, I'd think. If I could get rid of the fat, look different, they would all be sorry that they'd treated me so badly.

With the benefit of hindsight and counselling I see this for the flawed thinking it was, a sign of low self-esteem. But back then I just wanted to feel in control of my life. So I set about controlling the one thing I could at that time – the way I looked.

14. The 'New' Fiona

The first cosmetic surgery company I called told me they wouldn't take me on for a weight-reduction procedure because I was too heavy. By then I was eighteen stone and a size 22. The next clinic I rang, Advanced Cosmetics, was a lot nicer. They asked me to come in to talk to them and I was given an appointment at their office on Lower Leeson Street. I went there and talked to a surgeon called Samy. Dr Samy Malhas. He examined me and said that he could do a tummy tuck for me. It'd take pounds away and give me a flat stomach.

I went off to think about it. I had some money set aside. Nothing was stopping me. I worked hard and didn't drink or smoke. When the children were young I had put them first. Now they were older I could think about spending some money on myself.

For a week after that Advanced Cosmetics rang me regularly, telling me of available dates, dropping the cost every time. They even said they'd throw in some liposuction. I was sold. I made the appointment for a week later. 'This is it,' I thought. 'My big change. The new Fiona.'

I lied to my employer and co-workers and friends, not telling anyone what I was doing in case someone tried to talk me out of it.

I was taken into the clinic in Stillorgan the night before

the procedure and treated like a queen. I had no qualms and went ahead with the op. I really did think it would be a whole new start for me.

When I woke up after surgery the next day I felt like my body was on fire. I couldn't move with the pain. I was cut on both hips, my belly button was moved, my ribcage was bruised to bits from the liposuction and the pain was really bad. I didn't care though. It was worth the pain. I had a flat stomach. It was all that mattered.

It was a long recovery from the surgery; I had to wear awful support knickers that went right up under my boobs and down to my knees. Each day the pain eased a little more. I was starting to feel good and to gain some confidence.

I was asked to be a female bouncer at a club in Dublin. It was to be a new career path for me. I dyed my hair blonde and felt I was standing up to the world. Things were looking up.

When I went back to Advanced Cosmetics for the after-care, I talked to the girls working there, telling them how good I felt, how the tummy tuck had helped me feel better about myself and that it'd led to my job as a female bouncer. They asked me if I'd do some promotional work, modelling for them. In return I would get free Botox and other treatments. Boy that gave me a boost! I didn't have to be asked twice. They arranged a photo shoot and sent a taxi to pick me up. My picture appeared in a magazine.

I really enjoyed the whole experience. It felt good. I started to look at myself even more, thinking, 'Well, what if I change other things?'

After months of working as a bouncer in Dublin I went

to work for a security company nearer my home. This was the new me. 'No one will mess with me again,' I thought. I was looking better and feeling confident. I went back to Advanced Cosmetics, back to Dr Samy. He smiled when I walked in.

'Fiona, what can I do for you?' he said.

'Samy, have you seen *The Swan* on television?' He looked at me, confused. I explained that *The Swan* was a programme on television about ugly girls in America who are given surgery to help to turn them into beautiful women. I wanted to be like that. I wanted to be transformed. I wanted to have my pick of men, not be grateful when one picked me.

My next operation was to have my breasts reduced. I also wanted them perked up and given some shape. I'd paid €5,500 for my tummy tuck and didn't regret it for a minute. How would I feel after this? 'The sky's the limit,' I thought. I would get a reduced price for the breast op because of the modelling I'd be doing for them. So I was booked in. This time I didn't lie to people, I was upfront, telling them what I was doing. The operation cost €4,500. I didn't care. I flew through that surgery and was back in work, stitches and all, shortly afterwards. I had gone from a 44DD to a 38DD. I was looking great. I felt great.

Every time I went to the clinic I would have Botox and fillers. I even had permanent make-up done. People were starting to talk about me.

I was featured in newspaper articles. I did breakfast television, got the nickname 'The Glam Bouncer'. I revelled in it. Working as a bouncer I was getting asked out all the time but I said no. Saying no was power.

Operation number three was on my thighs, to cut away the fat. It cost another €4,000. Did I care? No. I was on a roll.

The security work was going great. I moved up the ladder pretty quickly, got my own team of men. I had a very good boss who had faith in me. It was so good for my confidence. I was also earning more money than I ever had. So I went to have my legs done. Dr Samy again. I was pretty sore after it, stitched right up to my private parts. Doing my job was hard and painful in the weeks afterwards but I didn't mind. More photo shoots followed. I even appeared in a TV documentary series about the Irish economy called *In Search of the Pope's Children* presented by the broadcaster and economist David McWilliams.

I was then asked to be head bouncer in a nightclub in Wicklow. I jumped at the chance. Things were getting better all the time. There was one problem though. My scars got infected. I was in a lot of pain. I had to drive to the clinic every day to have my dressings changed and the dead skin cut away. Still I didn't care. I was months recovering but I loved my job and it kept me going.

I was getting respect. Men weren't sure about me at first when they saw me; they thought I'd be a pushover. The lads I worked with were a great crew. They knew I could handle myself and more.

I'm looking at myself in the mirror hanging in the hall. I was passing it when I caught sight of myself. I did a double take and am now standing here, eyeing myself critically. I look so different. I can't believe the transformation. I have a shape now. Curves. I turn this way and that, pleased with myself. It's made such a difference to my self-esteem.

It's given me such confidence. People look at me differently now. I like that. I love the way I feel, like I can take on the whole world.

I started to worry about putting weight back on. I would panic about weight gain when I ate, wondering if I was undoing all the work and the pain I'd gone through in having the tummy tuck. I was in the clinic one day doing a photo shoot with the owner, a woman named Halina Ashdown-Shiels. I mentioned to her my fear of putting on weight. She told me she was about to introduce the gastric banding service to the clinic.

Now this was exciting. I wanted it, made her promise to let me know when I could have it. I didn't care about the cost. About a month later I was told I could have the stomach banding. It would cost €10,000. Again I didn't care, I wanted it so badly. I told them I'd do anything they wanted, chat shows, magazines, newspapers, I wanted this operation. So we went ahead with it. In May 2006, just before I turned forty, I got my gastric band fitted. I was the first person in Ireland to have it done.

My job was still going well, I was head bouncer at the nightclub and a security team leader in Croke Park at big matches and concerts. Then I was asked to take a security team to the Ryder Cup when the major golfing event came to the K Club in Kildare in September of that year. It was a very prestigious event and it was considered something of a coup for Ireland to have landed it. It was a big deal for me. It was exciting. I was in demand. I was still getting phone calls from Larry but I was staying well away from him.

My kids decided to throw a fortieth birthday party for me at the end of May 2006. They had organized a limo to pick

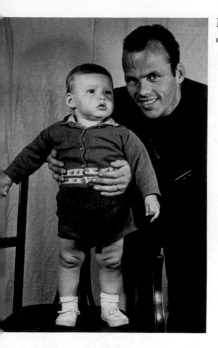

My father, Patrick O'Brien, with my older brother, Austin, in the mid-1960s.

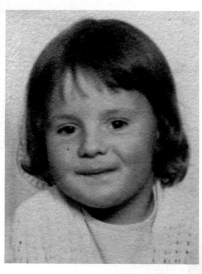

I'm five in this picture. My abuse started around this time.

My Confirmation. My mother wouldn't let me choose my outfit and I hated this dowdy get-up.

Me (left) and my sister Laura in our Dominican Convent uniforms. I'm about fourteen.

A cousin's visit to our house the day of her Confirmation (she's in the hat and bow tie). The picture includes my mother (on the left), father and younger brother, Richard, at the back. I'm in the pink-and-white dress. My father claimed I dressed provocatively in my teens but pictures show me looking very modest.

Laura's Confirmation. She's in the white cap. I'm on the left with Christine beside me and Richard in front. We look like any other happy family but our home was full of tension and aggression. Around this time I was treated for a sexually transmitted disease.

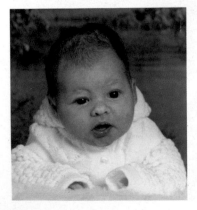

I had this picture taken of my first daughter, Kelly, in spring 1985 when she was just a few weeks old. Allowing my parents to adopt her was the biggest mistake of my life.

A family gathering in Bray for our father's sixtieth birthday in 2000. I'm at the extreme right at the back. Christine is beside me and Austin beside her. To the front – left to right – are Laura, my parents and Kelly. The four others at the back are aunts and uncles.

Me at my fattest. On holiday with Paddy in Lanzarote in 2001.

Deasún's Communion in 2003. Either side of me at the back – Paddy, Lewis and Kristel.

A small selection of the coverage I received when I became a 'poster girl' for cosmetic surgery in Ireland.

Ireland's TOP woman's weekly!

December 20, 2006

woman's way

REAL LIFE

'I got plastic surgery for Christmas'

Fat, frumpy and single... these women were

Drastic sur

Addictive: above, Fiona Doyle after €43,000 worth of surgery. Left, Fiona before her transformation

I SEE MYSELF AS A WORK IN PROGRESS

FIONA DOYLE, 41, a nightclub security spe...

SO HAPPY, I NEA

DEIRDRE WHELAN, 43, a...

Two months later, in October 2004, I decided

16 Plastic Surgery: Not Just for the Beautiful People »

Loads of ordinary Irish women are having loads of cosmetic surgery. Niamh Horan met some of them

Ireland on Sunday, May 21, 2006

Meet the first Irishwoman to have pioneering weight

I ate my way to hell but my and of hope ll let me live

By Georgina Heffernan

A fully adjustable new stomach

FOOD ADDICT Fiona O'Brien was on suggestion point. Her marriage had broken down in ...

COVER STORY

Plastic is fantastic for affluent new breed

No longer confined to celebrities or the super-rich, plastic surgery is becoming an increasingly acceptable lifestyle choice for Irish men and women

After the surgery, my confidence shot up and I felt I could take on new challenges. I really enjoyed my developing career in security and was delighted to be asked to take a security team to the Ryder Cup when the major golfing event came to the K Club in Kildare in September 2006.

THE K CLUB | STRAFFAN | COUNTY KILDARE | IRELAND | SEPTEMBER 22-24, 2006

The Ryder Cup Matches 2006
Brought to you by this foursome

My wedding to Jim in Barbados in December 2006 was a very different experience to my first wedding almost exactly seventeen years earlier. While I was a little lonely not having my children there, the first one had been lonelier, even with my parents and siblings present. My cousin Nicola is my bridesmaid in the picture below.

WHY?

...ONY OF WOMAN RAPED BY HER ...NSTER FATHER ... AND THEN ...TRAYED BY THE JUSTICE SYSTEM

By Niall O'Connor

RAPE victim Fiona Doyle was today asking one question – why?

Why was her evil rapist father, who abused her for 10 years, allowed to walk free?

There was widespread public disbelief after Patrick O'Brien was given bail despite pleading guilty

girl on the eve of her First Holy Communion and continued the abuse for another ten years.

Despite being sentenced to 12 years in prison, O'Brien walked free after a judge suspended nine years and allowed bail pending an appeal.

There were strong calls today for the court authorities to "fast-track" his appeal process amid fears that it could be months until he ends up in prison.

Ellen O'Malley Dunlop, of the Rape Crisis Centre, told the Herald: "For the victim's sake, I truly hope we are not facing a situation ...

From grief to relief. Over the course of a few days in January 2013 there was massive coverage of the awful outcome of my father's initial sentencing hearing and the judge's subsequent decision to revoke bail and send him to jail.

▲ IN DEMAND Kristel O'Brien yesterday

GARETH McNAMEE

MY PAEDO DAD

Abuse victim Fiona thanks public for support

RAPE victim Fiona Doyle has told how she felt "pity" for her sex beast father when she saw him in court.

The 47-year-old finally got justice this week as evil Patrick O'Brien was jailed for the decade of abuse he inflicted on her.

But she said she was filled with pity for the man who ruined her childhood.

The mum also told how she thanked the support of the country after O'Brien was allowed to walk free from court on Monday helped carry her through.

She told the Late late Show: "To woke up on Tuesday morning and listen to the outpouring of the public, the Facebook page, the people of Bray, the nation, everyone.

"They carried me. It's hard, [I felt] pity [in court]."

Meanwhile, Ms Doyle's daughter has called for a probe into how her mother's horrific plight was ignored by officials.

Kristel O'Brien revealed how her mum ended up in hospital as a young child with a sexually transmitted disease but no action was taken.

The 26-year-old told RTÉ's Pat Kenny Show: "Why wasn't something done? Where were social services?

"That's what confuses us, there must be records."

Mr O'Brien added her mother's battle for justice started nearly a quarter of a century ago.

Ms Doyle lodged an unofficial complaint to gardai in 1989 but it fell on deaf

There's no record of her complaint to Garda in 1989 being logged

DAUGHTER KRISTEL

COURT Patrick O'Brien and his wife Bridget at Monday

Wife avoids prison visit

By RORY TEVLIN THE wife of sex beast O'Brien did not visit her husband in jail following his first night behind bars.

Bridget, who has stood by the monster, did not show up at Arbour Hill Prison yesterday to visit the sicko.

O'Brien, 72, was locked up on Thursday after his bail was revoked by Justice Paul Carney.

The judge was roundly criticised earlier this week when he released the paedophile on bail pending an appeal.

O'Brien faces three years behind bars for the horrific attacks on his daughter between 1973 and 1982.

Despite standing by her man in

Here I am with the Taoiseach, Enda Kenny, when we met in February to discuss the issues arising from my case. The picture includes Deasún, Lewis, Kristel, my husband, Jim, and Paddy. I am giving the Taoiseach a crystal angel to bring him blessings!

With Mary Flaherty, CEO of Children At Risk in Ireland (CARI), at a fundraiser in May 2013. CARI is a voluntary organization that provides specialized therapy and support to children, families and groups affected by child sexual abuse.

me up. Lots of people turned up and I was delighted. They gave me a great party; it made me feel so proud. But I was still a little sad. I was on my own, having no one special, apart from my children, to share it with. Was this to be my life?

Physically I was happy with myself. My gastric band was working great and I was losing weight. I also had my eyes lifted. But, as time went on, all these treatments couldn't take the loneliness away, or lessen my sense of isolation.

15. Finally Meeting My True Love

One night in 2006, shortly before my birthday, I was working on the door of the nightclub in Wicklow. I was chatting to some of the girls I'd gotten friendly with, inviting them to my party, and a guy I knew to see asked jokingly if he could come too. I said yes, laughing, but walked away thinking, 'I hope you do come, I like you.' He didn't show up.

A week or so later I was asked to do a photo shoot for a newspaper dressed as Marilyn Monroe. The story was due out a week later. The weekend before it was due to be published the same guy walked into the club. It was a Saturday night. I'd lost weight and was feeling attractive. I felt I was doing great, in control, everything was normal. I was honoured to be taking a security team to the Ryder Cup. I was even allowed to pick my own team and to organize the security checks. I was busy; no time to think. I had booked a holiday for my family, planning to go to Portugal in September. I was also handling the management of the security team for three other pubs as well as being head bouncer in the nightclub. I joked with this guy, called him a 'cheeky fecker', asking to come to my fortieth birthday party and then not turning up. His name was Jim Doyle. He asked me when my birthday was and I told him: the 27th of May. He said his was the same day and he'd been celebrating his own birthday that night. 'Yea, right,' I replied. He pulled out his driver's licence and showed me his date of birth. The 27th of May, the same date as mine. Only I was six years older than him.

He asked for my phone number. He wanted to take me out the next night. I was working as a security supervisor at a big match in Croke Park the following day. My main team was working the Hill 16 terrace with a few guys around the other levels. I was tired; I hadn't got home from the night-club until four in the morning and was back up out of bed to go to Dublin early. I was due back in the nightclub again that night. That afternoon I asked some of the lads I knew on Hill 16 if they knew a Jim Doyle. I got some good reports back and as I was talking to them I got a text from him, asking me to meet him that night for a drink. The lads encouraged me to go, one even offered to cover for me at work. They knew I hadn't been out for such a long time and that I hadn't had an interest in any man for about eighteen months. I agreed to go.

It was about 5.30 p.m. by the time I got home and I wanted to see my kids and spend some time with them. After that I was so tired that I went to bed for an hour. I was due to meet Jim at nine but just couldn't do it, I was too tired. So we changed the time to ten o'clock and I still didn't make it for then. I arrived at about 10.45 p.m. He'd waited for me. I was so impressed. We had a drink and went into the club where I worked. At least I was there, so I could monitor things.

Jim and I got on very well. We even got up for a dance. As we were dancing though, a fight broke out. By instinct I grabbed a guy, brought him down the stairs and threw him out. I went back up to Jim afterwards and asked him if we could go downstairs to the front door and chat while I kept an eye on the lads. He didn't mind so we went and sat in the beer garden.

As we were talking the guy I'd thrown out started to shout abuse at me, calling me names and roaring obscenities. I got up to approach him and he spat in my face. That was it. I punched him one in the nose. He disappeared off. Talk about making a first impression!

We continued talking. A while later another man came around the corner and started shouting at Jim, calling him names for hitting his son. He turned out to be the father of the lad I'd thrown out and punched. The father was going mad, calling Jim all sorts. His son turned and said, 'Dad, it wasn't him, it was her!' Well, everyone in the beer garden just cracked up laughing. I felt for sure I wouldn't see Jim again after that, but he didn't seem bothered at all.

We drove back to my house. I liked him and we got on well. We talked all night until about six in the morning. I told him about my operations and about some of my past. Jim left for work. He had to be in by seven. I went to bed. Good job I'd told him about my operations as that story about me, dressed as Marilyn Monroe in an evening gown, was in the *Daily Mail* the next day.

Jim sent me a text that day saying he'd seen the paper. I was very tired but I wanted to see him again, so when he asked me to meet him that night I said yes but I had to make it late as I had to meet the lads that I'd picked to do the Ryder Cup and get the vetting forms signed. So we met up late that night.

It was the start of something very special. We didn't want to be apart, we wanted to know everything about each other. Jim agreed to come and work with me at weekends so we could see each other. He was just six months out of a thirteen-year relationship. He had two young daughters whom he adored. He had them overnight at weekends and sometimes during the week as well.

We wanted to spend all our time together. In August we had a wedding to go to and I was looking forward to it. Jim gave me butterflies, I loved him and I knew it. We had a deep connection. I told him everything. All about me, my past and my father. We were able to talk about everything.

He brought out the best in me. My kids loved him too. In August we were booked into the hotel for the wedding. Jim got a loan of a jeep for the weekend; he was really treating me special. That morning he collected me and we went to the church. After the church we went to the hotel for the reception and I met some of his friends that I didn't know. We all got on great and had a laugh.

After dinner I went for a walk with Jim's friend's wife. We were gone for about an hour and when I got back Jim wasn't there. His friend said he was off bringing the bags to our room as we were staying the night.

He came back a short time later and we decided we would head to the room for a break and a rest, so we went to the room and, when we were outside the door, Jim said, 'Close your eyes.' I did and he led me in, and when I opened my eyes he had written on the bed with rose petals: 'Will you marry me?'

He went down on one knee. He had a ring. I couldn't

believe it. I knew then this guy was so special. I said, 'Yes, I will marry you.' We went back down to the wedding to celebrate. I rang the kids to tell them. They were thrilled. I was so happy. The next day we went home and my kids had a party organized in the house for us.

I didn't see my parents until after the weekend. I went up to my mother's to show her my ring. I was so excited but when I showed her she just looked at it and said, 'It looks like Kelly's.' Kelly had been engaged for about a year at that stage. My ring was nothing like Kelly's. I felt my mother was so jealous. I got flashbacks of my first wedding and there and then I promised myself she wouldn't get the chance to ruin this for me; in fact I didn't even want her and my father there.

I went to Jim. I was a bit upset. We talked and I told him I didn't want my parents at my wedding, that I wanted to go away, just the two of us, so that people wouldn't ask questions. We were planning to wait a year and then go with the kids but six weeks later a spanner was thrown in the works. I discovered I was pregnant.

I'd been losing so much weight as a result of the gastric band that I hadn't suspected anything. I just couldn't believe it. I was still working as a bouncer. I wondered what would happen with my job. I went around in shock for about a week, not knowing what to do.

Even before I told Jim I knew that, no matter what, I couldn't do anything other than keep the baby, with or without him.

When I told him he couldn't have been nicer about it. He was a bit shocked at first but we both knew we wanted to be together, nothing would change that. We decided we wanted to live together and get married before the baby was born, so we looked into it and arranged to go, just the two of us, to Barbados to get married in December.

In early September I had a scan. We were told I was having a baby boy. We decided to call him Jack, after Jim's Uncle Jack. I had to go and get my gastric band loosened so that I could eat enough for me and the baby. When I told the cosmetic clinic about Jim and the baby and us wanting to go away to be married they asked if they could do a big story about the two of us. I agreed.

Shortly after the *Sunday World* newspaper did a centre-piece on Jim and me. I was called 'The Glam Bouncer' again. They wrote about my operations, my job, me meeting Jim and being pregnant and about us going off to be married. But deep down I knew this was all hiding the real truth. Despite everything, I still felt deeply sad. Nothing seemed to fix those feelings of how ugly I felt inside, no matter what I did or how hard I tried.

I got busy with plans for our wedding. I bought my veil first. It caught my eye in a shop; I loved the gold embroidery on it. Then, instead of a dress, I bought a full-length skirt in a champagne colour to go with the veil and had the bodice and top made to match by a dressmaker, using gold material I'd found. I loved the off-the-shoulder design and the drop sleeves. In early December we went off to get married. I felt so bad for my kids. I wanted my boys to walk me down the aisle; I wanted Kristel there helping with my make-up and dress. I felt guilty too, it was Jim's big day also and he deserved to have his family and friends there with us.

He didn't get that because of my past and my Big Dirty Secret. I just couldn't face getting married close to home and the possibility of something coming up that would ruin our day.

I'm going to have to do my make-up again. I've been crying and I've messed it up. It's the morning of our wedding. I want to be happy, I am happy, but I miss my kids. I want them here with me on my special day. I feel they should be here. We are going to be a family. They've been on the phone already, wishing me luck. I miss them terribly.

I hope someday Jim and I will get our big day with our kids, my four boys all walking down the aisle with me. I hope we'll get to renew our vows and do it all again with everyone there. Except my parents. Jim shouldn't miss out because of my past. I reach for a tissue. I don't want Jim to see me upset. He's been so good. I don't want to spoil this day for him.

I felt very lonely that day, even though I was happy with Jim. I did cry a few more tears but Jim tried to make it special for me. Paddy had given me a Westlife CD and the track 'The Rose' was played as I walked towards Jim on that sunny day. We were married by a pastor whose name I don't remember. Jim cried as he said his vows. We asked two people we met to be our witnesses. I was five months pregnant by then. We spent ten days in Barbados. We stayed in a four-star hotel and it was beautiful but I wasn't in the right frame of mind to appreciate it. I hid from Jim how sad I really felt. Jim went without so much for me.

We did a lot of talking while we were away and decided that, after Christmas, we were going to move away to north Wexford to be closer to my Uncle Des and Aunt Alice, who had moved near there. I knew my marriage wouldn't work if I stayed near my parents. Jim couldn't bear to live close to them. We had to move, to have any sort of life.

I finished up in my job. I couldn't do it any more, being pregnant. We put my house in Oldcourt up for sale. Over the years, I'd bought it out from the council. We found a house to rent down the coast and moved the first week in January 2007. Deasún was only eleven. It was hard for him, he had to move schools.

My mother told Paddy and Lewis they could move in with her and my dad and the boys decided that's what they'd do. They wanted to stay in Bray. I thought my mother was only interested in the rent my boys would bring in. It broke my heart. I didn't want them there. The boys didn't know about my abuse. They knew there was bad feeling between me and my parents over something in the past but they didn't know what. That was my fault; I couldn't bring myself to tell them.

16. Settling into Our New Life

For weeks I couldn't settle in my new home. I kept going back to Bray to check on my boys. I got diabetes and ended up having to inject myself three times a day. I wasn't allowed to drive much. The kids came to see me as often as they could. One day they were down and thought I was in bed asleep all day when in fact I was in a coma. I was rushed into hospital. I was so unwell that the hospital decided to perform a Caesarean section and Jack was born on 10 April 2007. The doctors had warned me that I would have to make sure I didn't have any more babies, so during the operation I had my Fallopian tubes tied. I was very sick. Having the stomach band saved my life, the diabetes would have been much worse if I hadn't had it as it restricted what I ate, keeping my weight down and my blood sugars even.

None of my immediate family came to the hospital. Why did I expect they would? Jim and his family came, so did my aunts and uncles and, of course, my children.

On the day I was discharged from hospital I made Jim drive me to my mother's to show her my new baby son. Again, I can't explain why. Jim wasn't happy with it at all. Looking at it now, who could blame him?

I started to notice a change in Jim in the following months. Was all this getting to him? It must have been hard to handle. But there was something else I couldn't put my finger on. I loved living in north Wexford and it was starting to feel like home. Jack was six weeks old when I decided to go back to work as a bouncer. I rang my boss and was given a job in a nightclub in a town near to us.

After a few months I discovered Jim had a drink problem. It was a shock to find this out now. Was I a dope? Or were my own problems all I thought about? Jim had gone on a couple of binges and hadn't come home. I decided to confront him. I told him I would leave with Jack; I wasn't going to rear my baby around alcohol. He knew I meant it. He said he didn't want to lose me; we loved each other too much.

We wanted so much for Deasún and Jack, I wanted a proper family and we were going to fight for it. He went to see the new local GP and, with his help, Jim gave up the drink. He did that for me, for us. I was so proud of him. I felt so wanted and needed by him.

Jim went to visit the doctor a few times; he liked him and got on well with him, so I decided to go with him on one of the visits. We talked about Jim first but then the doctor turned to me and asked me about my past.

I just said, quite casually, 'Well, I was abused by my father.' The doctor was taken aback by this. He asked if I had ever done anything about it and I told him about going to the gardaí sixteen years earlier but that nothing had happened afterwards. He asked me to consider going to them again. I was kind of surprised. I hadn't thought about it before.

*

Kelly had a baby. I fell to bits the day my first granddaughter was born. My mother told me I wasn't to go to the hospital. I started crying on the phone. I didn't get any sympathy from her – as usual, she didn't seem to care. I just wanted to be accepted as the grandmother. I wanted them to stop shutting me out but all I did was make a fool of myself. I didn't see the baby until about two weeks later.

I couldn't bring myself to go to Bray but Kristel said she'd go up with me. Paddy wasn't in my parents' house at this stage; he'd had a row with Kelly and they told him to leave. I was so heartbroken for Paddy but now he saw them for the people they were. I needed to get Lewis out too.

I would visit and get to hold the baby and take sneaky photos of her. I felt I had to be careful because if I did or said anything that I shouldn't I wouldn't get to see my first grandchild.

I tried after that first visit to go to Bray at least once a week but I struggled with it. My father was going in and out of hospital and they'd phone me asking me to visit him there. I did it, but it was getting harder and harder for me to bury my past.

One day I called into my parents' house when Kelly's little one was just a toddler running around. Kelly was at work and my dad was in the sitting room with the fire blazing. My mother shouted at the little girl to go and see her granddad. God, I had to leave, it brought back too many flashbacks. I went home in tears to Jim. What if my dad started on her? The same fears I had had about him abusing Kelly came flooding back. I couldn't just ignore this, I had to do something.

It was 2010. My father's seventieth birthday was coming up and the family were planning a big party in their garden. Some weeks before the party, my mother had a fight with Kristel because she had been invited to the full day of a family wedding and Kelly to the evening part only. I was so upset with what she said to Kristel that I called her to defend Kristel. My mother said Kristel wouldn't be allowed go to the seventieth birthday party. I said she didn't want to go and that I didn't want to go either, why would I go to the party of the man who'd abused me?

My mother replied, 'Well, you did well out of him, didn't you?' and she hung up.

I couldn't talk. I was in shock at my mother saying that to me. How could she be so callous? I started to cry. Jim was there and I told him what was said. He just put his arms around me as I sobbed. I was so upset.

I heard nothing for weeks. The party went ahead. My sister Laura came from England and my dad's brothers turned up along with his sister. They were told that I was saying mad things again. I was denigrated and called crazy.

Kelly got in touch by text. I asked her to just mind her little girl, to just promise she would protect her. She made it clear that she didn't believe what I was saying about my father. So did my sister Christine.

I didn't know where to turn, I was getting very depressed. I remembered the writing I'd done years before, when Kristel was fourteen, things I had written down about my situation when I couldn't talk to anyone about it. I got it out and went to my friend who said she'd type it up for me and email it back to me.

In the meantime I talked a lot to Jim, about what would happen if I went to the gardaí again, how would I handle things? I was getting angry texts from members of the family on a regular basis. I was upset much of the time and worried about my little granddaughter.

One day I was sitting at home on my own, in tears, and I rang the Rape Crisis Centre in Dublin. It was so hard telling them my story. They gave me a phone number for the Sexual Assault Unit at Harcourt Street Garda Station. I didn't ring them that day. I kept the number and looked at it from time to time over the next few weeks.

Meanwhile my friend had typed up what I'd written and emailed it to me. I sent the email to Kelly and some friends, even to some of my cousins and aunties and uncles. Some of them got back to me. They were very shocked. I was surprised by the reaction but when I thought about it, people didn't know, did they? I would say I was 'abused' but I never went into the detail. I never told anyone, properly, what had happened to me.

Time passed. I went backwards and forwards about talking to the gardaí. I wanted to do it, then I didn't. I drove Jim mad. It was frightening, the idea of handing over my story – my life – to the gardaí.

Finally I decided to send the email to the gardaí. What did I have to lose? It couldn't get any worse. I spoke to a female officer, Michelle, in the Sexual Assault Unit in Harcourt Street, and told her I was forwarding her the email.

I told our doctor I'd done it. I felt like I was cracking up. He suggested I see a counsellor. He also offered to give me medication to help me but I refused.

Jim and I were still doing a lot of talking. He was being great. I felt like it was all getting on top of me, that everything was such a mess. Why couldn't I just keep my mouth shut?

Kristel was suffering too. Somebody from the family rang her workplace, accusing her of talking about their business outside of work. It looked like people were now lashing out at me through my daughter and putting her in a terrible position. I felt so bad for her, being dragged into this mess. Jim would find me in tears so often during that time.

I was out shopping one day, feeling down, everything going around in my head, when I bumped into the woman who'd been the manager of the Resource Centre when I'd lived in Bray. She was now in charge of one in Gorey. I told her what was going on with me. Here I was, in the middle of Dunnes Stores, pouring my heart out. She listened and said she would be able to get me a counsellor. She could see I was in a state and she promised to phone me. She kept her word and the counselling was organized. Thank God it was.

I had to wait weeks after talking to Michelle, the garda, for her to get back to me. In those weeks the hostility I got from my family made it a lot easier to go ahead with it all. Outsiders were also getting involved – friends of my parents, extended family, other relatives – and I got some unpleasant emails and texts from people calling me a liar.

I think it was because they thought I'd backed away with my first complaint to the gardaí nearly twenty years earlier. They thought if they put pressure on me I would back down again. Little did they know; I was a different person now. I wasn't going to be put off this time.

*

Jim and I and my kids discussed everything over that Christmas in 2010. Ireland was in the grip of a major cold spell and we'd had snow and ice in north Wexford for three solid weeks. Getting about was difficult, which was why we spent more time indoors together.

It was also the Christmas that Kelly got married.

I've hoovered the house from top to bottom. Washed walls. Scrubbed bathrooms. Anything to take my mind off the fact that my daughter, my first-born child, is getting married today and I am not allowed to be there to be a part of it. She doesn't want me there and my family doesn't want me. It hurts so much. It's like a big ball of hurt inside me, crushing against my ribs. It's mid-afternoon now, she'll be coming out of the church. Is Kelly thinking of me at all? Is anyone there thinking about me? Are any of them thinking of the hurt I'm feeling? I wonder what she looks like. I mustn't think about it. Too painful. Too hard.

The details of the wedding were all kept quiet, but not quiet enough. In the end, I heard all about it. He, my father, walked her down the aisle. My sister came from England for the wedding. Aunts and uncles, friends went. No one got in touch with me. None of my kids were invited or the aunts and uncles on my mother's side. Anyone who supported me wasn't welcome.

For me, though, the pain was turning to anger. Anger at my mother and father. It made me more determined to see this through, to take another chance at getting someone to listen and believe me this time. And, more importantly, to act.

Eventually, after me hounding the gardaí over Christmas, I got word that my case was being sent to Kill of the Grange Garda Station to be investigated. It was a little light at the end of a long tunnel. Did this mean that they could see some truth in what I had written?

The case had to go to Kill of the Grange because that was the garda station nearest to where I'd lived when I was growing up. Wasn't that where I'd made my previous statement twenty years earlier? I couldn't remember for sure but I thought that if it was, maybe they'd find my old complaint on file.

The complaints against Kristel at her workplace continued into early 2011. She had to explain to her manager there what was going on, what the motivation was for the accusations that were being made against her. The gardaí were involved. Her managers were great and saw it for what it was.

Kristel also got calls from Christine that January saying that a member of the family had tried to commit suicide and that it was all my fault, because of the things I was saying. I felt so bad. She was getting all the crap because I'd changed my phone number and they couldn't contact me. I'd had to. The texts I was receiving were too upsetting. Now my daughter was getting it instead. I was worried about the person who had tried to commit suicide; it was someone I loved to bits. I thought about going to visit that person but I knew I couldn't. It would just make things worse. So I left it. It bothered me greatly.

It was sometime later that I got a call from a detective called Darragh Phelan to say he would be investigating my case. I went to meet him in Bray Garda Station. I was pretty nervous but Jim came with me. It was scary; after this there would be no going back.

Darragh was a young guy, a family man. He went through the stuff in the email I had originally sent Michelle in Harcourt Street. We talked about doctors who had treated me as a child, about hospital records, dates, etc. He said he'd be in touch with forms for me to sign to give permission to get my records released. We talked about who in my family would be prepared to make statements.

He told me that this was his first 'cold case' as he called it. I made a joke of it but initially I thought, 'Oh shit, he doesn't have much experience.' He made me relax though and gave me faith. I had a good feeling about him. I felt he would do his best for me.

Some time later Garda Phelan told me a search had been done and no record was found of me having spoken to the gardaí before. That was truly upsetting. What had happened to it? I was starting to realize that maybe there hadn't been an investigation into it before, after all. Maybe, when gardaí spoke to my mother and father back then, they had convinced them I was mad and making up stories. What if that happened again? My mind was in a whirl. Panic set in. *What am I doing?* Jim tried to reassure me, telling me not to worry, not to get stressed. He had got good vibes from the detective and believed that it would all work out.

It was time to start thinking about what other steps I needed to take. I decided to send my solicitor the email about my past and to try to get an appointment with him. Also the welfare of my granddaughter was still weighing heavily on my mind. I'd been talking a lot about this to my counsellor and I needed to get in touch with social services to tell them my fears. I had to go back to the people who hadn't listened before.

I rang social workers a few times and left messages for them to contact me. I discussed this so many times with my counsellor and she knew how worried I was, so much so that she wrote to them herself and also rang them once while I was there. After about three weeks they got in touch and made an appointment for me to go and see them. I also got an appointment with my solicitor on the same day.

By now, I hated going to Bray. I was afraid of bumping into one of my family and what they might say. Also, Richard and his family had moved back to Bray but hadn't been in touch with us. This confused and upset me because I thought he believed me. I didn't know what I would say if I ran into him.

The social worker was a young woman, only about twenty-three or so. I told her my history with social services, about my concerns, and gave her a copy of what I'd written. She told me she would follow it up. It gave me a bit of hope that maybe someone was listening and would do something this time.

I then went to see my solicitor. I'd already emailed him my history and details of my past. I'd known him for over twenty years and I found this meeting very hard. As we started to talk I could see the shock on his face. I could see tears in his eyes. I started to cry. I always hated the reaction the details of my abuse caused in others. It was as if I were tainting others with my Big Dirty Secret. As if by telling another person I was drawing them into the awfulness of it. I was embarrassed to be crying in front of him.

I reminded him that I had told him before that I had been abused in childhood, when he was doing my divorce. I also reminded him that my ex-husband had been planning to use my abuse against me in trying to get custody of Lewis. I don't know why it all seemed like such a big shock to him. I suppose people don't always make the leap in their minds between the term 'sexual abuse' and the day-to-day reality of a little girl being mistreated, molested and raped throughout her childhood. I can understand that it's not something a lot of people would want to think about in detail, even when they are sympathetic.

I told him that I'd spoken to social workers and the gardaí before and no one did anything and that now I had to get the gardaí involved again and I needed his help with all this. I needed someone on my side who I could trust as I still didn't trust the gardaí.

He promised me he would help and do what he could for me, that I was to email him as things were progressing, and in the meantime he would write to the HSE for a copy of my files. I drove home exhausted that day, getting cross with myself because I hadn't asked him this or told him that.

I heard back from the detective, finally, in early 2011. I was to go to the Bray Garda Station to make my statement. My head was in turmoil, panic set in – 'What if I don't remember enough, how will I tell them it all?' I thought. It sounds stupid but I felt very lonely in all this. I had strange feelings and didn't know how to explain them or even why I was having them. I started to feel as though I was being taken over by this but still I was trying not to let on to Jim and the kids that it was all churning around in my head. Jim would ask me if I was OK, of course, and I would say yes but really I wasn't.

I would lie awake at night going over what questions I would be asked, what my answers would be. I'd stress about what details I'd be asked. I was worried because my memories would come to me of different incidents at different times, seldom in the order they happened. I could remember more about some incidents than others, like the time on Brittas Bay, my First Communion, the time we were all in the car and my father threatened to crash into the wall. Something would happen to trigger a particular memory sometimes. At other times they'd just come into my mind, unbidden.

The worry went on non-stop in the run-up to my making a statement. I'd suffered at other times in my life with panic attacks, pains in my chest when my feelings would overwhelm me. Now they were back, worse than ever.

Jim came with me the day I went to make my statement. Paddy and Lewis met us to take Jack. While we were at the garda station I forced myself to have Jim in the room with me. How could I go through this in court in front of strangers if I couldn't do it in front of my husband? But I wondered how he would feel when he heard all the awful details? How would he be with me the next time he went to touch me? Would he be thinking of my father? How would he deal with all this?

By the time we got to the garda station I was completely worked up. The detective made me feel a bit at ease. He started first to talk about the letters I had sent to doctors, hospitals, the HSE and my previous social worker before starting the statement. I surprised myself, when I was talking about certain things, how good my memory was. Like sometimes I could even describe the clothes my dad had been wearing. I wasn't asked too many embarrassing questions or asked about anything I didn't want to talk about. We only got halfway through and the detective said we'd have to stop and finish it at another appointment the following week.

When we walked outside the garda station things started to hit me. The strongest feelings were ones of shame and feeling dirty. Feelings that I'd been trying to suppress for years. We'd been in there for three hours. I couldn't believe it. And to think I was going to have to go through it all again the following week. I wasn't sure how I could face it again.

We went to the park afterwards that day to meet the boys and collect Jack and as I hugged him it confirmed for me that yes, it had to be done. That night when we got home Kristel rang to see if I was OK and to give me words of encouragement. Texts came from the boys. When I got into bed and cuddled up to Jim he was no different with me. He didn't treat me like I was dirty. It gave me the strength to face the next appointment.

The following week I was still panicking. I was still nervous and anxious. The detective told me the HSE couldn't find my file and that he'd written to the social worker but hadn't got a reply. He wrote down and confirmed old addresses and we finished my statement. It took another two hours. I felt drained after it. He told me he'd be taking statements from Des and Alice next and from another aunt.

Weeks would go by and I wouldn't hear anything but I kept up the barrage of emails. Des and Alice's statements were taken, things were moving but not fast enough for me. My solicitor was still writing to the HSE for my files. The HSE wasn't answering the detective's letters. My first statement to the gardaí still hadn't been found, nor were the names of the gardaí who'd taken it. When I heard that I had little faith that it ever went to the DPP.

As time progressed I hounded Garda Phelan with emails, asking questions about letters, times, dates, replies, I was determined that I would know everything this time, I wasn't going to let things go over my head like the first time I went to the gardaí. But I did have times, in those weeks, when I'd wonder if it was all worth it, if I could keep going.

Will it be different this time? What if it isn't? What if I'm putting myself, Jim and my children through all this and the DPP decides again that my father has no case to answer? 'God,' I think, 'it'll kill me if that happens.' It's so hard talking to the gardaí about my Big Dirty Secret. Saying aloud the awful details. I hear myself saying the words as I make my statement but it's as if my voice is coming from someone else; I can hear it, but it's outside my body. Maybe I should just leave it. I can't though. Not this time.

The counselling has helped me see a lot. How bad decisions and wrong choices I've made throughout my adult life are the result of me having been abused as a child. My life has been shaped by it. I am defined by it. I am certainly damaged by it. If I am to have a chance at a different kind of life, if I am to heal so that I can have a chance at happiness with Jim and my children for the rest of my life, then I have to deal with this. I need to have it acknowledged that what was done to me was grievously wrong. I want to be vindicated.

17. The Long Road to Court

It seemed like I was hitting brick walls everywhere. No one wanted to help or get involved. Those were the times when I really felt like throwing in the towel.

My former social worker told Garda Phelan she didn't remember me. Even though she'd seen me regularly for months. Even though I have voluminous correspondence with her name on it. Letters signed by her to me and copies of letters she sent to others, trying to get help on my behalf. She'd been the one who'd urged me to make the first complaint to the gardaí and she'd been with me when I did. She'd got the council to rehouse me. She had written to the priest at the Marriage Tribunal in response to his queries about my suitability for marriage. In that letter she confirmed that she had regular contact with me from May 1988 to September/October 1988, periodic contact in 1989, and again from September 1990 until December 1992.

Garda Phelan had told me he was going to ask Richard to make a statement. He now got in touch to say Richard had refused and said that no abuse took place. He said Christine also denied that any abuse had taken place and that she was willing to make a statement to that effect.

I would get so down when I received news like this. But Jim would put his arms around me and encourage me to keep going. A lot of tears and sleepless nights followed. I'd just have to keep going now, I'd tell myself. Turning back wasn't an option.

Garda Phelan talked to my mother. I wasn't allowed to read her statement. I was just told that she said she knew nothing. She was asked about me going to hospital with genital warts and she said she remembered that but she didn't know how I got them because I didn't tell her and, if I'd gotten them from my father, wouldn't she have them too?

What people were saying to the detective was how mad I was and how out of control I'd been as a child. The story that had been trotted out so many times before.

When Garda Phelan started his interviews my father was in a hospice for pain management so questioning him had to wait until he came out a couple of weeks later. In the meantime the detective got the files from the doctor that I'd attended when I was young. The files confirmed that I'd been treated for genital warts when I was thirteen and had to be sent to hospital to have them removed.

Garda Phelan asked for a photo of me when I was younger to see if it would jog the social worker's memory. Maybe if she recognized my face she'd remember my case.

The week he was due to meet with my dad to take his statement the detective got a letter from my dad's doctor to say he was unfit to be interviewed, that he suffered with 'brain failure' and organ failure. The appointment was cancelled.

That August bank holiday weekend was my dad's seventy-first birthday. He went on the ferry to England. When I heard this I went mad. I think it was the first time I was angry with Garda Phelan. I rang him and shouted at him. I know it wasn't his fault but I was so frustrated. 'He's not fit to sit and talk to you but fit enough to go on the ferry to England,' I told him. He was going to his sister's in Wembley.

He calmed me down, explaining that the letter from the doctor wouldn't be taken as gospel, that the garda doctors would see him and they'd decide if he was fit to be interviewed or not. 'It just takes time,' he said.

'Time I don't have!' I shouted back. 'He's getting old; I will have no chance to prove I'm not lying if he dies.'

That was my big fear, that he'd die and I'd live out my days without ever having been vindicated. I felt sick with worry, wondering: 'Am I ever going to get through this?' It was all taking so long. I was also plagued with the feeling that I had no chance, that I'd never prove that I wasn't lying. The panic and frustration was so bad it hurt my chest. I needed to get away to sort my head out. I decided to go on holiday with Jack to my friend's in Malta, just to take a week away without thinking about things before I cracked up.

Jack and I went to the sun and we had a great week. I would take Jack to the beach on my own and watch him build sandcastles. The smile on his face gave me strength. Kelly had had another child at this stage and Jack made me think of the two grandchildren I didn't see. I imagined them there with us.

I knew I had to keep it up; I had to fight on. The truth had to come out for the sake of my kids, my grandkids and my future grandchildren. I was glad I took that week.

When I got home I went straight back to bombarding the

detective with emails and asking my solicitor where my HSE files were. The social worker recognized me from the picture, but didn't remember the case.

By November Garda Phelan had everything ready to send to the DPP to see if a decision would be made on whether or not to charge my father. He told me the decision would take about six weeks, so I'd hear just before Christmas. There was nothing for it but to wait.

Christmas came and went without me hearing anything. It never left my head. Sometimes I wondered if they'd forgotten me. I continued emailing and texting Darragh Phelan. The poor guy was sorry, I'm sure, that he'd given me his mobile number. He was very patient.

Meanwhile I would hear things about my family. Everyday stuff. My dad was still going in and out of hospital. I felt like I was such an outsider, just like before. But, unlike before, I was able to cope with it. I still hadn't told Jim's family or anyone at work about my abuse or about trying to get my father into court. I couldn't tell people in case the DPP decided not to proceed. How would I cope if that happened?

New Year 2012 came and went and still no word. Richard asked Lewis to be godfather to his new baby grandchild. It really upset me. Richard had refused to give the gardaí a statement and said he knew nothing about my abuse, but now he was reaching out to my son. It struck me that if my children were seen to be close to family members who were denying my story, then it might look like they didn't believe me either. The more I thought about that, and questioned Richard's motives in approaching Lewis, the more I worried about being paranoid, but I just couldn't help it. I had a fairly unpleasant text exchange with Richard.

A week later I kept receiving messages from Richard to get in touch. I just ignored them. Finally, sitting in the car at Courtown Harbour with Jim by my side, I dialled my brother's number. I was so nervous. But when Richard answered his tone of voice was warm. He said he wanted to speak to the detective, that he couldn't live with this any more, that he believed me and needed to do what was right. I trembled, holding the phone. *Do I believe him?*

I rang Garda Phelan and he was excited at the news, felt it was a breakthrough. He told me he'd make himself available to meet Richard the next day at Bray Garda Station.

Afterwards I sat in the car in pure shock. I was in tears. Jim couldn't believe it either. Maybe now I could get somewhere. Maybe now I could prove what was done to me.

I didn't sleep that night, there was so much going around in my head. Angry feelings surfaced again about how I'd been treated over the years. I couldn't show my anger now though. I needed to stay calm and hold my nerve. I watched the clock all night and into the next morning.

I know I'm driving Jim mad. I can't help it. Time is going by so slowly. It's torture. If this could just be done. If they just had Richard's statement. It would strengthen my case so much. Oh God, don't let him have changed his mind. The detective is to ring me to let me know when it's done. Why hasn't he rung? Surely it must be done by now? I feel sick with nerves. I'm tormenting Jim, pacing back and forth, demented, going over things endlessly, asking how could the DPP say no to charging my father now that my brother had come forward, and my aunts and uncles, pointing out that they had the records from the hospital now and the only thing missing is the HSE files? They still can't be found.

Finally, I got the call from the detective. Richard had given his statement and it supported my story. I couldn't believe it. I rang him and thanked him. He asked me not to say anything that would get back to the family as he needed time to sort himself out and figure out how to handle it. I promised I wouldn't say anything. The sense of relief was huge. I can't explain it.

Richard and I kept in touch after that and we talked a lot. He said he didn't know a lot of what had gone on. It was sometimes frustrating talking to him about the past but I had to remind myself how much younger he was and that there were things he probably just wasn't aware of.

We kept it quiet for a few months that we were in touch. I even went to visit Richard at his home during that time. As we talked Richard got braver and, in the end, he let our parents know he was in touch with me. I offered to go and confront them but they wouldn't agree to see me.

In all those months there was still no word from the DPP. I carried on hounding the detective with emails and questions. Didn't they realize the effect it was having on my life?

Richard was talking to everyone by now. At one stage he told my father that I wanted to meet with him to talk. My father asked Richard: 'What if she wants to record it?'

Richard told Christine that he'd made a statement to the gardaí and talked her into meeting me. Then he had to talk me into meeting her. I was wary and turned up at the meeting in his house equipped with a hidden recorder. I wanted a record of what was said.

The three of us thrashed things out, going back and forth over stuff. Christine said she believed me. That was a very emotional moment for me as we had not talked for so long. She was going through her own feelings about the past, worried about how all this would affect her children.

Both of them said how reading the email outlining my abuse had brought back so much to them of the bad side of our childhood. I was stunned. Angry too. All I could say was, 'Well, what the hell do you think it was like for me?'

Though they said they believed me – Christine even recalled my mother taking me out of my bed and putting me into bed with my father – I couldn't help feeling they wanted me to drop my complaint. We talked about our parents and Christine said she couldn't turn her back on them. We talked about Kelly too and Christine said Kelly just didn't want her children – my grandchildren – to be exposed to any of this. She also said she didn't think our father would ever admit abusing me in court.

At the end of our meeting I was shocked when Christine said she would give a statement saying what she knew. I drove all the way home in tears, my mind racing. I didn't know whether to be furious that it had taken this long for them to talk about what they knew, or grateful that they were finally speaking out.

Looking back, I suppose their heads were wrecked too. If you grew up with parents like ours it could be very hard to think straight and they were still able to play people off against each other.

I rang Darragh Phelan the next day to tell him Christine was ready to talk. He was pleased; he felt it was another step in the right direction in the case.

Christine got on to Laura in England and she agreed to come home to speak to the detective too. Things finally got moving. I found those couple of weeks hard; there were a lot of texts and phone calls back and forth.

At last things were all set. Laura was coming home and she and Christine were going to go down to the garda station. Garda Phelan had also been on to me to say that Richard and I were to come to the station as the DPP had asked him to ask us a few extra questions. Things didn't go as planned though. A few days later Christine was in my parents' house and told my mother she was going to make a statement on my behalf. My mother acknowledged that my story was true. Kelly's husband overheard the conversation and that night they and their children moved out of the house. My father was getting well and truly backed into a corner.

18. My Father's Admission

My father finally crumbled. Now that his behaviour was out in the open he realized he couldn't hide. Richard got a call to go to my parents' house. There was a lot of talk but the upshot of it was that my father agreed to go to the garda station to admit all that he had done. Richard phoned me to tell me to ring Darragh Phelan to set up a time. An interview was arranged for the next day at eleven o'clock.

Needless to say I didn't sleep much that night either. I was back to watching the clock, willing the hands to go round. It was nearly lunchtime the next day when I got the call to say my father had made his statement and admitted everything. 'Now you can breathe a sigh of relief,' Garda Phelan told me. He wouldn't go into what my father had said, but he indicated that he had shown no remorse. I think he was in shock at how casual my father was about it all.

As word got out that my father had admitted my abuse I began to get calls from people, expressing their shock. I wanted to scream, 'I told you all this twenty years ago, stop acting shocked now!' But I had to keep quiet.

Jim and the children were fantastic throughout this time. Sometimes when I had to go to Bray – which was always hard for me – Kristel came with me and stayed with me.

It was tougher with my siblings. We had quite a few conversations in the days and weeks after my father admitted what he had done. You might think that would be the end of it, but families are more complicated than that. I felt like I was walking on eggshells because I needed their support and yet I would sometimes become really angry that they just didn't seem to get it as far as I was concerned.

Laura was coming home a few days after my father's statement and Garda Phelan still wanted to interview her. When I saw her, she was full of anger about our parents. She felt terrible about the damage they had done to our relationship, about her not having believed me. We hadn't spoken in a year. Her feelings about our parents were fairly black and white: she just didn't want to be near them. Christine and Richard, on the other hand, each had a more complicated set of feelings. They couldn't seem to get it clear in their heads how they felt about me or the situation or our parents. Christine in particular was terribly concerned about our parents' welfare and she also worried about the impact of the whole thing on her own family. I desperately needed them to speak to the gardaí so I had to hide my frustration and disappointment when I could see they were wavering.

Finally, on 1 May 2012, all four of us talked to Garda Phelan, Christine and Laura to give statements and Richard to go through some follow-up questions on his statement. There was some follow-up with me too. I wanted the detective to tell me more about what was in my father's statement, but he couldn't. I found that so unfair. Why couldn't I know? I was told that all the statements and follow-up material were to go back to the DPP and I had to wait again for their deliberations.

We left the garda station and went down to a pub on Bray seafront for a chat. It felt strange, being in their company, all four of us getting along.

Kristel arrived after work and so did Paddy and Lewis. I was supposed to stay up in Bray again that night but went outside and rang Jim, asking him to come and get me. I didn't want to stay another night in Bray. I was delighted when he arrived with Deasún and Jack. I went home that night with them. I needed to be at home to sort out my head.

It was back to the waiting game. It was July before I got the call to say my father was being charged. He would be facing roughly eighty charges in all. Due to the courts being closed for the summer though, he couldn't be brought before a court until September. That meant he couldn't be charged until August as he could only be bailed for four weeks.

So this is it. Finally. It's going to happen. We are going to court. Not just that but, because my father has made a statement admitting he'd abused me, there will be no need for me to go into the evidence. I won't have to stand up in court and go through the awful, shameful details in front of a load of strangers. I won't have to be cross-examined. I'm really glad about that. I don't trust myself to react well, not to lose my temper, if my father's defence counsel were to question what I was saying, as if I shouldn't be believed. I feel like I'm on a roller coaster of emotions. I thought I'd be elated, getting to this point. Instead I feel strangely flat.

About two weeks later I rang Darragh Phelan about having a meeting. I needed to know the exact charges my father was facing, and the procedure, what would happen. We met in Deansgrange Garda Station. Jim came with me. I wanted to know how they came up with the number of charges. The detective explained that my father had admitted to raping me from the age of seven so it was one rape charge for every three months and the same with the sexual assault charges.

Again I asked for a copy of his statement and again he explained that I couldn't have it. To placate me he read out some of my father's statement.

It started with him being asked how old I was when the abuse started. He said I was about seven. The detective told him I'd said I was younger than that. My father was adamant that he was right. The detective asked him how he could be sure and my father told him it was because I was bleeding at the time. The detective asked him how he'd known that and he told him he'd known because he'd put two fingers inside me. It was awful, hearing that. I cringed in the seat. I was so embarrassed and ashamed. And also amazed that he was so ignorant and stupid, that he thought anyone would believe a child of seven had already started her periods. Trying to make his actions sound less serious – on the grounds that I was physically mature when he started to abuse me – was just pathetic. The detective then told him I'd said the abuse took place nearly every day; that it was as routine as having dinner. My father replied, 'Ah no, no, no. Not at all. It was probably every second day, or once a week. I knew I shouldn't be doing it but I just kept on. I was hard on Fiona because of the way she dressed. She was a right one for the boys. I don't understand why I did it; she was very good to us.' It was so shocking, hearing that. I had to get out of there. I needed some fresh air.

Jim and I went outside to the car and we just sat there in shock. I started to cry. 'I can't do this, Jim,' I said. 'I can't have this said in court. What about my boys? I can't have them listen to this.' I sobbed my heart out as Jim drove home.

Weeks went by. August came; my father was going to be charged shortly. I got my boys together and sat them down, explaining to them what my father had said. It was the first time I had told them to their faces, not written it down and handed it to them. I had to tell Kristel as well. I found it very hard to deal with. I couldn't get what my father had said in his statement out of my head. I was really sorry I'd asked the detective to read it to me.

Kelly and her family were now living back with my parents. She and my mother brought my father to Bray Garda Station on 13 August. He was charged with seventy-two offences, thirty-six of rape and thirty-six of sexual assault.

A few days later I went to England to spend some time with Laura to talk about things and for us to get to know each other again. I got on great. I was really nervous about going but while I was there I started to relax. It was like home away from home.

While I was there we also went to see our Aunt Bernie, my mother's sister. She was delighted to see me. She too felt very bad as she'd believed my mam and dad's stories about me. As we were on our way to see her we drove past the area that we had lived in when we first went to England, and

Laura had some flashbacks of my dad shouting and screaming that he would drive the car into the wall. Laura was
angry at herself for turning against me. An uncle also spoke
to me during that trip and said he was sorry too for believing the stories my mother and father told him. All these
people saying they were sorry – it should have made me feel
better but it didn't. I found it hard to listen to.

When I got back from England, Jim and I decided to
have a night out. We needed a break and we needed a laugh,
so we decided to go to see the comedian Tommy Tiernan,
who was appearing in a local hotel. That night I got a call to
say my father had gone into hospital. I was devastated. Not
because he might die, but because I might miss my day in
court. Luckily he was OK.

19. 'Guilty'

We'd decided to travel to Dublin the night before the court case. The hearing was to be in Dun Laoghaire District Court. I was asleep in the hotel room when my phone woke me. It was Kristel to say she was on her way out to have dinner with us. I'd been asleep for just ninety minutes. We had a takeaway in the hotel room and Kristel was all chat, talking about exams she was doing a few days later and an upcoming holiday in France with her boyfriend, Paul, and friends. I knew she'd come just to check if I was OK. When she left I soaked in a hot bath. It was strange how relaxed I felt compared to the rest of the week. At 11.30 p.m. I was asleep and I slept all night. I woke at 7.30 a.m., shocked that I'd slept like a log; I didn't expect that I would. I'd had so many sleepless nights over all this, now here I was on the morning my case was to be heard in court, having slept soundly.

Richard had said he wanted to attend court so we picked him up. As we walked to the courthouse I saw my mother and father sitting outside. My father was leaning on his walking frame. Richard laughed and said, 'He wasn't using that last Thursday when I saw them at the slots on Bray seafront.' I could see our parents were shocked that Richard was with me.

For one split second I want to turn and walk away. The fear I used to feel as a child is back, bubbling up inside me. I am sick with nerves now. I have to remind myself: I'm an adult now, a strong woman, these are two old people. I've waited for this day for so long, wanted it, longed for it. I've imagined it in my head a thousand times. Today is the start of a new chapter in my life. Today I begin to leave the old Fiona behind. I step out of the shadow of the abused child. I stand up and say: 'What was done to me was wrong.' I seek accountability. I seek justice.

After a few minutes people started to move into the courthouse so we went in to get a seat. My father went to get up, made a big show of moving very slowly and shaking as if he were having trouble holding his own weight. He walked very unsteadily and people ran to open the double doors for the old man. He and my mother sat behind me. The detective was in the courtroom. After a few minutes the detective called me outside. He explained that the Book of Evidence was ready to be served, which I hadn't expected. He also explained that the judge was a woman, Judge Claire Leonard, who was very thorough, and that the wording in the charges had to be changed.

I asked for a copy of the Book of Evidence but I was told I couldn't have one. I've learned since that the complainant in criminal cases isn't entitled to see the Book of Evidence. It's not the done thing. Anyway this was the State's case against my father and not mine, a fact that was to leave me feeling sidelined as it progressed.

My Uncle Des arrived at the courthouse. It was nice to have him there. He was determined to be there, to show my mother I had the support of her side of the family. We sat there until one o'clock. It was strange sitting there with my mother and father behind me. I could hear their breathing. At one o'clock we were told to go for lunch until two.

After lunch my mother and father were sitting in seats to the side and I sat on the opposite side, facing them, so they would have to look at me. After an hour, finally, his name was called.

Again, he made a big deal of standing up and moving his walker towards the judge. At one stage I almost felt sorry for them, these two old people. She would wince every now and again as if she were in pain. This was my mam and dad. *It shouldn't be like this. I am their daughter. How must it be for them?* But my pity didn't last very long. I had to remind myself why I was there.

Judge Leonard asked my father his name and told him that he faced seventy-two charges. His solicitor stood up to ask for legal aid for senior and junior counsel. I was surprised. Why two? But the judge said no, she would only allow a senior counsel. The detective then served the Book of Evidence on my dad. The judge decided to go through all seventy-two charges. The room was quiet for a long time. I started to think about a book I'd read, *Click, Click*, about three Dublin women, the Kavanagh sisters, who were abused by their father as children. They'd gotten him to court in 1990. They talked about how they felt in court, about how it was as if their feelings didn't matter. Things hadn't changed much in the years since, I thought. I was the victim and there I was, sitting for hours in the room with my abuser. Shouldn't that have been considered?

His solicitor then asked that my father not be named in the media. I wanted to scream, 'I am here, isn't it up to me to decide that? I don't want this; I want to name and shame him!' But the judge granted the request and forwarded the case to the Central Criminal Court in Dublin. At 3.40 p.m. we walked out of the court.

Outside Richard said, 'My God, this is moving fast.' I just felt angry at the fact that my father seemed protected. I know that wasn't the case, it was to ensure he had a fair trial, but it felt as though yet again my feelings didn't seem to matter.

We dropped Richard home. I was feeling numb. My phone was beeping like mad, friends and my kids wondering how it went.

We got home about 5.30 p.m. It had been a long day and I had a bad headache. Jim went to the shops and came back with a bunch of flowers for me. God, he's such a good man. What was the day like for him? His mam had rung, and his sisters. They all knew what was going on by now, of course. They all called to offer me support, telling me to hold my head up. My sister Laura sent me a lot of nice texts. It was good to have her back in my life. But, throughout the whole day, I kept looking, looking, looking for some sign of remorse, some sort of look of sorrow from my father. When am I going to learn, eh? I'll never get it.

Apart from that time when I invited him to my house for coffee and he told me he'd ruined my life, there had been no expression of regret. And he'd even denied after that day that he'd said that.

And in my immediate and extended family, things continued to be difficult after that first court appearance. Family turned on family. Cousins were not talking and my kids were not invited to a twenty-first birthday party of a cousin they had been close to. I got calls worrying about my parents' welfare from people who should have known better.

Laura rang me from England and told me that my next court date was 22 October. It was the first I knew of it. She had heard it from our parents as my father had got the call a couple of days before I heard. I was livid. I got in touch with Garda Phelan. He said he hadn't known the date himself. He was off work, but as soon as he was back he texted me to explain. He said the case was up for mention only on that date. I got angry and sent him a text saying I didn't care how trivial he thought the next date was, I wanted to know, I shouldn't be hearing it second-hand from England. I had said that I wanted to be at every court appearance, no matter what. I felt disrespected. I thought that times hadn't changed at all; didn't they think this was hard enough without me being treated as if I didn't matter?

In the next few weeks I got a visit from my mother's sisters, all telling me I had their full support. One brought me a present and they all kept saying they were there for me. I could see the guilt they were feeling. I told them it was important to me that they didn't feel that way; there was nothing they could have done. If one of them had asked me, growing up, if I was being raped, I would have said no. I couldn't risk saying anything, could I? I never wanted to upset my mother or make her angry. Their support meant the world to me and the messages from my cousins on the Burke side of the family have been incredible.

It's different on my dad's side though. At this point there was no support from his family. Perhaps understandably. For now, they were keeping their distance.

The hardest thing I'm having to deal with is the news that Lewis is leaving the country. He applied for a job in Las Vegas and got it. He's waiting on his visa now. I'm so upset but I don't want him to see it. Boy am I an expert at hiding my feelings! I want the best for my boys. I will help in every way but the thought of him moving away is so hard. He will do well; I know he will. I am just being selfish, wanting him here. Either way he won't see how upset I am. I cried myself to sleep the other night, thinking about him leaving. He sent me a poem on Facebook:

> *A mother is special, she is more than a friend.*
> *Whenever you need her, she'll give you a hand.*
> *She'll lead you and guide you in all that you do.*
> *Try all that she can just to see you get through.*
> *Good times and bad times, she's there for it all.*
> *Saying head up, be proud and always stand tall.*
> *She'll love you through quarrels and even big fights,*
> *Or heart-to-heart chats on cold lonely nights.*
> *My mother's the greatest that I've ever known.*
> *I think God made my mother like He'd make his own.*
> *A praiser, a helper, an encourager too,*
> *Nothing in this world she wouldn't do.*
> *To help us succeed she does all that she can,*
> *Raised a young boy now into a man.*
> *I want to say thank you for all that you do,*
> *Please always know, Mom, that I love you.*

Boy that made me cry! And proud; so proud that he can say that to me. I also felt guilty because I should be enjoying my last few weeks with him, not worrying or stressing about court cases. He's moving in at the end of the month to spend the last few weeks at home with us. I have read that poem a good few times and it makes me sad too. Sad that I can't say anything nice like that about my mother, nothing at all.

I rang Richard on the Friday night before court to arrange to pick him up. He told me he'd been down at the slots that afternoon on Bray seafront and my mother and father were there. My father went up to him and started to moan about the fact that the taxi to court is €100. You know, I thought I couldn't be shocked any more but they always manage it. As if the cost of getting to court was his only worry, not the fact that he is in court for raping his daughter.

Richard also told me my dad's sister has booked to come home from England for Christmas with her husband and son, so they must be very sure he's not getting locked up for Christmas.

Despite what he told me, the idea of Richard having this casual chat with my parents really bothered me. I just can't get my head around the idea that my siblings can still have a fairly normal relationship with our parents. It feels like a betrayal although I know it's not meant like that.

Over the weekend Garda Phelan rang to tell me my father was going to plead guilty. There would be sample charges, one of rape and one of sexual abuse. They pick out one sample of each charge. This was good news but it felt strange at the same time. I started to panic. *Has he made a deal? What's going on?* A thousand things were going around in my head.

On the Sunday night I took a sleeping tablet. I had to stop the thoughts, had to stop my head spinning. It worked. On the Monday morning, 22 October, I got up at six, got ready, and we headed to pick up Jim's sister Lisa, then on to Bray to get Richard. Traffic was heavy. We got to the Dublin Circuit Criminal Court at ten o'clock.

The courtrooms are on the second floor, past the coffee shop, and just as we got up the stairs my mother and father came out of the coffee shop, him on his walking frame. The same feelings flooded me straight away, my childish emotions. I had to try to shake them away. Garda Phelan came over to me, which made my mind switch back. He then rang the DPP's office to say I was there, and the DPP's counsel, Monika Leech, came down to meet me. She explained that because my father would be pleading guilty we would go straight to a date for sentencing. She also advised me that after he had pleaded guilty the papers could name him if I was OK with that. Even though I had thought before that I just wanted to name and shame my father, I said now that I was just not ready for it. My emotions were all over the place and I was trying to take it all in. I could feel myself starting to tremble.

They told me to go into the courtroom and sit on the left-hand side. My mother and father were sitting in the hall outside so I thought I'd get in before them. Paddy had arrived as well so we went on in. There was a good few people in court. It wasn't a closed court, which surprised me. Next I saw a barrister leading my father in. He guided him over to where I was sitting and put him in the seat in front of me. Jim shouted, 'Don't fucking put him there!' The barrister looked at me; I think he could see the shock on my face. He moved my father away to another seat.

The court went through a few other cases and then my father's name was called. A court clerk read out the charges and, just as his brother and his wife walked into the court-room, my father replied, 'Guilty.'

I close my eyes. My body feels like a block of ice. There it is. 'Guilty.' I've just heard it. One single word that I've waited so long to hear. An admission of grievous wrongdoing. These are the charges and my father has just admitted that, yes, he did rape me and sexually assault me for over ten years when I was a child. I wasn't mad, or bad, I was telling the truth. I can feel Jim's hand squeezing mine as my father says it. I squeeze his back.

Judge Paul Carney remanded my father for sentencing on 14 January 2013.

And that was that. Short and sweet. My mother and father turned to leave so I held back. The detective and Monika Leech came up to ask me if I was OK with things. I said yes but really I was thinking, 'Why do I have to have this hanging over me for Christmas?'

Outside the court Paddy decided to give my aunt – my father's sister-in-law – a piece of his mind. His opinion of my uncle didn't leave much to the imagination. She looked shocked and I felt sorry for her. My uncle came over then and he looked pale. 'What do I do? He's my brother,' he said. I wanted to shout, 'Well, I am your niece, your flesh and blood too!' but I didn't. Why didn't I just say out loud what was going on inside my head? Instead, I asked them to come for coffee. They were going to but Paddy just made them feel uncomfortable so they left. I stood there feeling quite sad. 'What a broken-up family,' I thought. 'It can never be fixed.'

20. Extract from My Journal . . . Piecing Together the Past

I've been in therapy for two full years now. I found myself thinking the other day, 'When will I stop coming here?' The truth is that it can never be fixed. I can never be fixed. I do see things differently though.

I started writing down my story properly thirteen years ago. Mad, eh? But some answers have been found, some sense has been made of some things. For example, why did I get a beating if I forgot to rinse out my pants, why did my mother react like that? It sounds awful but I believe it was because she didn't want to see the trace of my father in my pants. Sick and twisted, I know.

Since my father has been charged people have been saying to me, 'When he is locked up you can get on with your life.' Really, though, it doesn't work that way. I will never stop having flashbacks. I will never stop smelling that smell. Kissing will never stop being a problem for me. So this is me, my life. It will never stop. Never a week will go by without me having a cry. The sense of loss will never go away. My lost childhood. The damaged relationships in my family. Years that I'll never get back and bonds that may never be repaired.

I worked out why I first told someone what was going on, that time in Holles Street, when I was pregnant with

Paddy in May 1988. I couldn't understand at the time why it happened then. Why did I crack then after keeping quiet for so long? Well, I figured out the answer. Kelly had turned three in March that year and it was getting to me. I was becoming increasingly worried about her welfare, knowing she was being reared in a house where a paedophile lived. My father.

I get angry and so full of pain when I am with my counsellor. Why didn't my teachers notice? I wrote before about how good I was at hiding everything but really the signs were there; I was quite withdrawn, more absent than present at school, I never had homework done, books were never paid for, and then there was the doctor. I was taken to him for headaches, brought to him with genital warts, for God's sake. A condition so bad I was hospitalized at thirteen for treatment. Then there was me going to school with a burst eye, with stitches, with fractured fingers. Why didn't the teachers, the hospital, the doctor, see anything? Oh and the shoplifting. I was caught a few times. I was such a sad little girl going around. And when I did tell people what was being done, nothing happened.

I made statements to the gardaí. I believed they would investigate what I told them but they didn't, because if they had they'd have found the medical records that have since emerged.

Then there was the second time I went to the gardaí. I was crying all the time, feeling like I was going to crack up, the amount of flashbacks I was experiencing doubled, I kept getting that smell, I wasn't sleeping, I didn't know why the panic in my chest kept coming. Now I do. It was because my granddaughter was coming up to three. History was repeating itself. I was as panicked as I'd been when my daughter was approaching that age.

It was at this time that the gardaí finally listened but it's been a long battle. How do those in authority feel, now that he's pleaded guilty? I wonder. My anger just turns to tears. I think of how many times backs were turned on me. I took a big chance going to the gardaí a second time; it was so hard, a war raging inside me.

I wondered how I'd handle it if they walked away again. How would I explain it to my kids, that no one believes me? But I had to go for the sake of my granddaughter.

I've been asked by my counsellor why do I think my mother wanted Kelly so much that she was anxious to adopt her. Only now do I feel able to give an answer. I think it was because she thought Kelly was my father's child. A lot of people have asked me that question, was Kelly my father's child? No, is the answer. An emphatic *no*. I am certain. She is not. And I am very grateful for that.

I hate the fact that my older kids know my mother and father and know what they did to me. I have Jack now, he's six as I write this book, and he doesn't know they exist. I wish it was like that for my other kids but at the time when no one would listen I felt I had to stay around, I had to pretend that we were normal, I had to hide my feelings and flashbacks with a lot of hidden tears, putting a smile on.

I would think of my father and get mental images of him on top of me, the smell of sweat, and my mother, her unkindness and lack of feeling. So I'd go to my room and cry.

Even when I tried to kill myself I told them in the hospital that no one had done anything to me. I wasn't able to. I was left to deal with it myself. My kids nearly lost their mother, I nearly died, but nobody seemed to be able to see what was going on inside me. When I think about how very low I got then I don't know how I survived. I did know how to be a good mother; I knew I loved my kids. They really did keep me going. I would look at them and think, 'If you only knew how I was really feeling.' Then I met Jim and discovered love, respect and support. Jim knew from the very beginning about my past but even he couldn't see how our lives would turn.

I never had any idea of the intensity of the feelings I'd have when my first granddaughter was born. We had moved away but the thoughts didn't stop, the sadness, the hurt. Jim tried his best and most of the time I could hide my feelings. I could hide the sadness. I would run a bath, get into it and cry when he wasn't around.

We talked a lot about going to the gardaí again, all the 'what ifs'; what if he dies and I don't prove that I haven't been lying? Wouldn't that be much harder? Over the past two years Jim has held me many a night. Sometimes it all seemed so hopeless. Weeks would go by and I wouldn't want Jim to touch me. Sometimes I'd be OK with a kiss; other times I couldn't even let him do that.

Showing my older boys what I'd written was so hard. The details; no mother should ever have to give her boys the details of her rape at the hands of her own father. Still, as time passed, some things did change. I stopped being so hard on myself. I did try to change things. I did try to get people to listen. I will never stop the feelings, the hurt, the smell, but I know I stood up for myself and in the end made people listen and got to prove I wasn't lying.

There is still one thing though that I haven't talked about. That's the shame I was feeling. The shame that made me keep quiet for so long, that made me feel dirty. The shame that still kept me from telling some people.

On 14 January, my last day in court, I will walk out without that shame. I will hand it back to my mother and father. It was never mine to carry. It's theirs. The tears will always be there, and the memories, and the sadness. But that deep, deep shame won't be there.

Despite everything my kids have turned out to be wonderful adults. Jim and I are hoping to renew our vows and he will get the wedding he should have had. We will start over. We will raise Jack with two loving parents who truly love each other. All this will be dead and buried. I will still have my problems. I wish my mind could be wiped clean but it can't so I will accept that this is me, tears, faults, failings and all. I won't shy away from it though. I won't carry the shame. I will tell the world how hard it has been, how so many people helped close the door in my face.

There are still nights when I lie awake going over details, going over the places I was taken to be abused, and an anger builds up in me, a frightening anger that stops me breathing, that makes me panic, and I have to cry to release it. It was this anger that would bubble up before my aggressive incidents with ex-partners. It scares me, what I am capable of when I am like that. I hide all this from Jim. He knows nothing of this. My first marriage broke up over all this and

I don't want to damage this one. It is far too precious. I do worry about how Jim will be if he knows. Will it be too much?

I think of Jim's family. This is when I feel dirty, that I'm bringing this dirt into people's lives. Some people will be lucky and get through life without rape or sexual abuse in their lives.

I was asked by the detective to prepare a Victim Impact Statement to be used in court. It will be my chance to address the judge and the court and tell them the effect my father's abuse had on me. I am so aware of how important this statement will be. Because my father entered a guilty plea to the charges, no evidence was gone into or will be now. So no one in that court, including Judge Carney, heard the details of what was done to me. This will be my chance to tell everyone present some of that detail and the consequences of it. I know that it could also, on some level, influence the judge's ruling when it comes to sentencing. So I'm deliberating over it. 'Agonizing' might be a better word. Finally, with some help, I feel I have it right. I play over and over in my head, me standing up in court, reading it out, waiting to see the effect of my words on everyone there, including Jim and my children.

After my last meetings with the detective, when we went over my Victim Impact Statement, I thought, 'Well, that's it until after Christmas. Everything is ready for 14 January so I don't have to think of it any more. I can put it out of my mind.' Really though, that wasn't to be. No one truly knows what I'm thinking. That every day I wake up and think, 'One day closer.' It won't leave my head. It consumes me. This just isn't fair, I feel, having this hanging over our Christmas. Lewis is due to go to America and I really want and need to enjoy having him around for these last few weeks.

During my latest visit to my counsellor I remembered something that has been playing on my mind since. I remembered that I used to rub the skin on my bottom, just below my tail bone, between the cheeks, with my fingers until it was like a carpet burn. Red raw. It would bleed and weep. It was to stop my dad from having anal sex with me. I did that for years. Why did I only remember that now? What other memories will come back to haunt me?

21. The Waiting Game

Paddy and Kristel each did their own things for Christmas, so this year it was Jim, me and the other three boys. We called to Jim's mam's on Christmas morning but came back to our house for dinner. As I looked around the table I thought, 'It's getting smaller, my family. Lewis will be gone next year.' His tickets were booked for 15 January. He had waited till the day after my case, bless him. He wanted to be with me for it.

I kept thinking about my mam and dad, wondering what was going through their heads. My dad's sister spent Christmas with them. She just didn't believe he had done it. She stayed in a hotel on Bray seafront. The amount of times it came into my head to drive to the hotel and confront her. But I didn't. I just could not get past these feelings of being aggrieved at family members who said they believed my father didn't do it. Even after he pleaded guilty. What would it take to convince them that I was telling the truth? Maybe nothing, ever.

We went to visit Des and Alice after dinner on Christmas Day and it just made me feel worse, like I didn't belong, I was not part of the family. I knew they'd go mad if they had any idea I was thinking that – they were always so good to me. I didn't hear from any of my siblings. Everyone was busy with their own families. Laura was home with her family and I didn't hear much from her. I tried ringing her on Christmas Day but they were playing cards and she couldn't talk. Herself, Richard and Christine together. God, I felt so out of it, so lonely, and I couldn't tell anyone because it didn't make sense to me, so how could I explain it to anyone else?

Laura arrived at my house on St Stephen's Day, 26 December, with her husband, children and granddaughter. She had refused to see my mother and father and was staying with her husband's family. I was so excited to have her around, I was like a child. After we talked though, I felt even worse. She told me everyone in Bray was going on as if nothing was happening, no one was saying anything about sentencing coming up. She said she couldn't really understand the others carrying on as if things were normal.

I told her how hard the past few weeks had been and how hard Christmas was. She read what I'd written in my Victim Impact Statement and we talked about some of my memories of the past. I felt a bit better after her visit. At least I had her in my corner.

Two days later she rang me from England to say that just as she was saying goodbye to her Christine told her the sentencing mightn't be happening on 14 January after all. Apparently my father's solicitor hadn't got all the files he needed. Again, it was the first I'd heard of it and naturally I was really upset. Had I gone through all this turmoil over Christmas, with 14 January looming in my mind, and now it mightn't even go ahead? When I got hold of Garda Phelan he confirmed that this was the case. This was hell.

This has been hanging over me all over Christmas and now there's

*a chance that he won't get sentenced on that day after all. It could be
adjourned for weeks. Don't they think I've been through enough? Why
prolong it for me? I feel like I'm cracking up. I spend my days endlessly
going over things in my mind until I think my head will burst. More
than anything I'm terrified that something will happen to stop him
from being sentenced at all. That after this long, torturous process,
justice will not be served.*

My job kept me sane. Jim and I worked long hours doing
security at the nightclub. It took my mind off things some
of the time. A few of those I worked with knew what was
going on but no one said anything or asked about it. I really
wish they had because the not talking made me feel so alone.
Again, I know that's contradictory, but those were my feelings. I think the kind of life I've had is responsible for all
these ambivalent emotions I have.

New Year's Eve was hard. Everyone in work was jolly,
wishing me a happy new year. I just smiled and said it back.
A few times I nearly burst into tears. I hadn't even sent
Christmas cards, I couldn't bring myself to. People's good
wishes were hitting a raw nerve with me, I wanted to shout
at people that in two weeks I go to court to have my father
locked up for raping me for over ten years.

*He's still my da. I don't have another. I don't have another family.
Guilt starts to creep in. Why did I start this? Why couldn't I just live
with it? Plenty of other people do.*

On New Year's Day I made a big meal for the kids.
Kristel was sick and couldn't make it but all the lads were
there. It took my mind off things for a while. To my surprise I got a phone call from Richard asking how my
Christmas was. He had already texted to thank me for

presents I'd sent his children. I told him it'd been hard with court hanging over my head. He said it was the same for him; he wasn't sleeping.

He told me he'd dropped into our parents' on St Stephen's Day and our aunt was there, my dad's sister, the one who was standing by him. She got up and walked out when Richard came in. I asked him if he said anything. He said no, that he couldn't be bothered. That just made me angry with him, for not confronting her. I get upset at the way they all tiptoe around things and don't talk about it.

Every time I think of the court date my stomach flips. No one really has any idea how I'm feeling. It's like I'm ready to explode. I'm fighting back tears all the time.

I went to visit Richard. He was sitting in the house on his own, playing the Xbox. He looked old and worn out. We talked about everything again. Who was on my side. Who wasn't. The usual. His partner arrived back while I was there and she told me Christine had said that many of the charges had been dropped. This had been said before – as if it meant that my father had been mistakenly charged. I was sick of trying to explain the concept of sample charges. That my father had pled guilty to two charges already and at his next court appearance he would plead guilty to another six to eight but that was just to cut it down, simply because it would take too long to read out all seventy-two charges. As they are sample charges, him pleading guilty means he's pleading guilty to all of them. I couldn't understand why they didn't get this by now. I left the house after an hour and a half totally drained, exhausted and furious.

*

It was Lewis's last week and I wanted to enjoy it but I couldn't stop fretting. I was struggling with all sorts of conflicting feelings and at the same time trying to hide them from Jim and the kids. Paddy was living back home with us and Deasún and Jack were back at school after the Christmas holidays. Myself, Paddy and Lewis went for a day out in Dun Laoghaire to visit my Aunt Pearl and we did a bit of shopping and went for dinner. It was lovely.

Around that time too I asked Des and Alice and cousins over for a meal with us all. Kristel and her boyfriend, Paul, were going to come too. I met up with my friend Lisa the night before to do some midnight shopping. We still did that quite regularly, especially when we were stressed. It worked for a while that night until I got out of the supermarket and checked my phone to find I had a text saying my dad had gone into hospital with a suspected heart attack.

There it is. What I'd dreaded hearing. A heart attack. Is it for real or is he faking it to avoid going to court? I don't know if I'm more angry at the thought of him faking it or at the thought of it being real. My heart is thumping. 'Don't you dare die now,' I think. 'Don't you dare.' The panic is subsiding, a slow-burning anger taking its place. I wanted to enjoy this meal with my family before Lewis went away. 'You ruin everything,' I think. 'Just like you always have.'

I got home and unpacked the groceries in a daze. 'What do I do now?' I thought. I went to bed but didn't sleep a wink. Sat up, the phone beside me, wondering what was going on. I had everyone coming to the house for a meal that day and I couldn't function. I felt cheated out of my day with my family. My father was the only thing on my mind. And I hadn't even got the news from a member of the family.

In the end, the evening we had planned was lovely and I managed to forget about things for a couple of hours. Unusually for me, I even had a few drinks – a few glasses of Baileys liqueur. The next day, Thursday 10 January, I got a call to say my dad was out of hospital. Phew. I breathed such a sigh of relief. We had four days to go before the hearing.

On Friday I had an appointment with my counsellor. I had a dose of flu and felt awful. We had a good chat though, about all the stuff that went on over Christmas and about my feelings.

Laura sent me a text that day to say she would be travelling through the night and would arrive on Saturday morning. She really made me feel supported. Yet I still felt ready to burst out crying, and I nearly did a few times with the counsellor. She asked me why I didn't cry over Christmas, just let it all out, and I told her I couldn't in front of my kids, that I felt I needed to stay strong for them. I couldn't have Lewis going away with a picture of me crying in his head.

I went home after the counselling session that afternoon still feeling crap and got into bed. At 5.12 p.m. my phone woke me. It was Garda Phelan. My heart skipped a beat, thinking he was ringing with bad news. He told me he'd got a call from the DPP and was told to ring me to warn me that my father's defence team were pushing to have the case adjourned because they hadn't got his medical files. I felt like screaming. It was so unfair. Just when I thought I was getting to the end they go and change it.

Garda Phelan kept saying sorry. I couldn't talk. I had a lump in my throat. I didn't dare speak or all my anger would have poured out. Laura was getting the ferry that night, my aunt had already arrived, and Lewis had delayed going to America. Kristel and Paddy had got the day off work. But I had heard just after Christmas that there was a question about not having certain files, so raising it now, right before the hearing, felt like game-playing to me.

I would have to turn up at the court on Monday and hope the judge would hear the evidence at least, and my Victim Impact Statement. I just had to keep my fingers crossed and hope. I hung up and cried, sobbed. How far can they push me? I picked up the phone to ring Laura, to try to get her before she left. I cried down the phone to her. She was shocked too.

Jim came into the room to find me sobbing. I told him about the call from the detective. I told him I couldn't take any more, that I felt like giving up. What difference would it make if I didn't go? Jim put his arm around me and said, 'You can't give up. Stay strong. Don't crumble now.' Easier said than done. 'You knew this would be hard,' he told me. I did but I didn't think I'd be pushed this far. I felt sick to the pit of my stomach. I'd two days left before the court on Monday to wonder. Wonder if I'd have my say or not, wonder if I'd be able to control myself in court if they adjourned sentencing.

Jack comes into the room. I rub my tears away but he senses something is up. He's only five but he's so clever. He starts kissing my head and pulling the covers up over my shoulders. He hugs me. I look at him and I think, 'He knows nothing about all this awfulness and he never will but he gives me strength. I will do this for him and for my other kids and my husband.' I will, you know. I will get through it with them. For them. I wipe away my tears. I will not be a victim. I am a survivor. Bring it on.

22. I Have My Say

Inside the court building the detective met me while everyone else was taken to a witness suite. He told me that they were still pushing to cancel today. He felt we should let it go ahead and be adjourned, because if I gave evidence that day and the case was adjourned for two months the effects of my Victim Impact Statement would be forgotten. 'I don't care,' I said. 'I'm doing this today. Take me in to the judge. I will confront him myself. It has to go on today. It will go on.' The detective looked at me. He sighed in resignation. 'OK,' he said, 'we'll try.'

I went back to join my family. The witness suite had sofas and was equipped with tea- and coffee-making facilities so we were able to make drinks. It was such a help. A liaison person from the abuse support group One in Four was with us too. I was called out again on my own by Garda Phelan. He said there was a problem. 'On your Victim Impact Statement you mention your brother's suicide. He wants it taken out.' 'He' meant my dad. My dad wanted it taken out. I was disappointed. I felt Austin should have been mentioned that day. He was a victim of our parents too. And why should my dad dictate what got in and what was left out? But I agreed. If that's what it took for the case to go ahead then I was prepared to let it go.

There was more. He also objected to two of the rape

charges being included. One was in the graveyard. I was sickened. He would take me up to the cemetery with him, he'd dig and clean up his parents' grave and then rape me in the trees around it. Why deny that? Was it that he felt shame about desecrating his parents' grave, but not his young daughter's body? The second one was the rape that occurred the time we went to the beach at Brittas Bay. Again I wondered, why that one? What difference did it make? Did he think all the sexual assaults that took place in the house – which he did not object to – were somehow not as bad as raping his daughter on a day out to the beach? Again I agreed to drop this one. Anything, as long as it went ahead that day.

As we were talking about it we got called in. The room was packed. Our case was called. I panicked a little. I was on my own apart from the One in Four support worker. My father's counsel stood up and asked Judge Paul Carney for an adjournment, saying they didn't have reports from the hospital. The judge denied the request though and said the case would proceed. My heart was thumping, my stomach churning. It was going ahead. 'Stay positive,' I told myself. My Aunt Alice and a friend had given me little crystal angels to hold and I also had a bracelet my cousin had given me.

It was happening. People's journeys to support me wouldn't be for nothing. I walked out, back to the witness suite, to tell them all the news. It's going ahead. They were pleased too. I told them to expect to be called in about twenty minutes. The detective called me out again, asked me who was with me and how they were related to me. The call to go down to the court came, as we'd been told, twenty minutes later. We made our way down to Courtroom Six.

When we got to the door the detective told me that only my husband, children, brother and sister were being allowed in. When I read my Victim Impact Statement everyone could go in. We entered the courtroom. It was nearly empty. My mother was there, with my father. His name was called and he stood up, leaning on his walking frame.

My father was led up to the dock. Seven more rape charges were read out and seven more charges of sexual assault. He pled guilty to them. The rape that took place in my parents' friends' house that night my mother threw us out was read out. That was the one where she walked in. It proved she knew. I kept looking over at her. Why I don't know. Looking for some sort of response, I suppose. There was nothing. She sat there, stony-faced.

Garda Phelan was called. I was aware of my mouth going dry. I'd never experienced that before. Jim must have sensed something, he offered me a mint. He put his arm around me. The detective started to give evidence, outlining the facts of the case. He read parts of my father's statement to the court and summarized other parts.

I can hear him but his voice is like an echo. The room is so still. He's talking about the violence, the names I was called, and relating my account of that rape in my parents' friends' house. The rapes in the car when my mother would throw us out of the house. It's like his voice is far away.

I fight back tears and try to swallow the pain I'm feeling. My poor kids. They're listening to this. That's the worst. Thank God we left Deasún outside. He's too young to be hearing this. The detective keeps

204

talking. On and on, he goes. Laying it all out. My Big Dirty Secret isn't a secret any more.

I looked at her again. My mother. Nothing. She continued to stare straight ahead.

Then it was my turn. I'd thought about letting someone else read out my Victim Impact Statement. I wasn't sure I'd be able to read it out myself. In the end I decided that I wanted to. I'd waited a long time to be listened to. I would tell them, in my own words, the effect of my father's abuse on me.

I had to walk around and up past my father to get to the witness box. I didn't look at him. I sat down and started to read but I began to struggle straight away. I admonished myself, thinking, 'Cop on, you have to do this.' I was aware of movement in the courtroom. Everyone who had come to support me came in and sat down. I didn't look up. I couldn't. I continued to read. I could hardly breathe and had to stop for a minute again. My voice was trembling and started to go. Tears started to fall. I nearly said, 'I can't do this.' I told myself not to look up, not to look at Jim and the kids. I cleared my throat and began again. It was an effort. I was torn between anger and sadness. I did it though. I got through to the end. As I stood up people began to clap. That annoyed Judge Carney, who ordered them out of the courtroom. My aunts and uncles stood up, they clapped again, hugged me and walked out.

I've included my Victim Impact Statement here so that readers will know exactly what I said when I stood up in court that day to explain how my father's abuse had impacted on my life. It's necessary to include it, I think, because a Victim Impact Statement is such an important part of any serious criminal case. Oftentimes, it is the only chance the victim in a trial has to tell their story and, particularly, to try to impress upon the judge the effects the defendant's actions have had on their life, and on their family.

This is what I told Judge Carney. This is what the prosecution and defence teams heard that day in court. This is what my family had to listen to. This is what my father and mother heard me say:

This Victim Impact Statement is to allow me to put across to you the effect the abuse I suffered at the hands of my father had on me.

The best way of demonstrating that is to give you one example from my childhood. A childhood robbed of its innocence and enjoyment by my father's actions. It was the night before my first Holy Communion. There was none of the usual excitement you'd expect in a family home where such a big occasion was to happen the next day. My mother went off to bingo, leaving me at the mercy of my father. Almost certainly knowing what he would do to me. And he did. My father raped me that night. In doing so he badly hurt me and made me bleed.

When he was finally finished with me I was sent upstairs to bed only to be met by my sisters who were annoyed that I'd gotten to stay up to watch television with him.

I remember lying in bed that night but being unable to sleep because of the pain. I was still sore and bleeding when I got up the next morning. My brothers and sisters were still annoyed with me that I got to stay up late supposedly watching television. I wasn't at all excited or happy that it was my First Communion Day. There was no excitement or happiness in my house. My mother dug her nails into me, pulled me around and called me names as she helped put on my Com-

munion dress. *Why was she angry with me? What had I done wrong? We went to the church and I looked at all the other children. They were smiling. So were their parents. Why weren't mine? I joined the other girls in the pew. The hard seat hurt. I was still so sore. I forced myself to smile.*

My abuse goes back as far as I can remember.

I was used for sexual gratification by my father. I was the helpless pawn in an evil marriage, used by both parents as a weapon to beat each other with. I was the cleaner, the babysitter, the cook, the protector of my younger brothers and sisters. I was cast in the role of the other woman in my parents' marriage.

I was told I was hated and not wanted. I felt worthless. I believed I deserved everything I got. I was isolated and ostracized by my brother and sisters. My childhood was taken from me. My virginity was taken and replaced with unlawful sex and beatings. I lost my self-worth and self-respect.

I craved love and affection and most of all protection. I couldn't trust anyone; my parents told people such awful lies about me to cover their tracks.

When they decided to leave the country I was left behind and moved into my father's bed full time until he was ready to join my mother in England. I was abandoned. I had to deal with pregnancy scares.

School was an added nightmare because of a lack of parental interest, no school books, poor attendance, no school friends. No one noticed my nightmare. I was taken into hospital with an STI that was so bad it warranted a three-day stay. Doctors, hospital staff, teachers failed to notice the signs. When I tried to stop the sexual abuse I would be beaten and have suicide threats held over me by my father so it was easier to co-operate and turn my feelings into self-hate.

My first baby was born in my first of many abusive and control-

ling relationships. I was only a year out of my parents' abuse and had no idea of how to be a parent myself. I had buried my abuse so well it was a secret even from me. I was bullied and cajoled into letting my parents have my first child. My insecurities and lack of self-worth led me to make the biggest mistake of my life, a mistake I will pay for for the rest of my life. My daughter in turn was told the stories of the awful person I was as soon as her adoption was finalized and she was turned into a weapon against me. I am now very much estranged from her and her children (my grandchildren). When my first child started to reach an age that I believe my sex abuse started I turned to social services (HSE) and in turn the gardaí in a bid to try to protect her. It was all to no avail. It all added to my struggle with being a parent. I struggled so hard. I had no self-respect, no self-worth; I felt I didn't deserve love, not even from my own children. My first marriage failed due to the effects of trying to raise my concerns, to no avail. It also led to a second, more serious, attempt to take my own life. I ended up in ICU for three days.

The poor choices I made had their own consequences for me and my children.

The psychological effects of my abuse led me to points in my life when I was at my lowest ebb. I truly felt that no one cared about me. I could see no way out of the deep emotional pain. That pain was often so bad it manifested itself physically over the years, in panic attacks, pains in my chest. An inability to sleep has plagued me for many years. The abuse has also led me to try to change all I could in my life — my outward appearance.

If I couldn't erase the memories of my abuse, if I couldn't see my father brought to justice, if I couldn't have a loving relationship then I would change the one thing I could — how I looked. So I went down the road of plastic surgery. I had many operations, which I see now was a form of self-mutilation. I have the many scars to prove it. Also, as far back as I can remember, I have hidden myself behind a mask of make-up. I wouldn't leave the house without it, my mask against the world to hide the real me. I also had a lot of anger issues over the years that interfered with me being a good parent to my own children, which I deeply regret. I feel it was largely as a result of the lack of belief and support from HSE and gardaí at the time. I truly loved my children but my issues clouded me and prevented me from being a good parent. I am sorry about the effect this has had on my children. This in turn would reduce me to feelings of shame and guilt. There is no way that these feelings are conducive to leading a healthy and normal life, but this was the hurt and pain I experienced each and every day since my abuse began. The manner in which I lived my life from the time I left home, the failed relationships, led to a hand-to-mouth existence for myself and my children. I struggled financially. I had little or no financial or emotional support, the kind that one would expect from a loving family.

This is the day that I thought many times would never come. I thought my father would die before ever being brought to justice and his abuse of me would die with him. That I would never be able to defend myself against the accusation of some family members, aunts, uncles, cousins, family friends and neighbours, that I was a liar. I am very glad therefore that we are here today. With these court proceedings finally it is being officially and legally recognized that a great wrong was done to me by my father.

No sentence passed by this court today can undo the enormous damage that my father has done to me. It is something I have lived with since I was a young child, and it's something I will have to live with until the day I die. It cannot be undone. My memory of my abuse cannot be wiped clean. How I wish it could.

Worst of all was the support and knowledge of my abuse by my mother and the resentment she had for me for coming between her and my father. A helpless child being cast as the 'other woman'. As if I had chosen to be abused. Her other response was to use the abuse as a means to gain freedom from her oppressive and violent husband. Bad enough to be abused by your father, but to have your mother complicit in it, while using it as an excuse to punish me, well how much worse can it get?

Today though I will walk out of this court without two things, guilt and shame. These court proceedings have taken the guilt away from me and given me my self-respect back. He is the guilty one. I did no wrong. I was a helpless child. He did what no parent should do: abuse their innocent child for his own gratification. I also leave here today without the shame that has been a part of me for over forty years. It is no longer mine to carry.

It has been acknowledged that I was wronged. My father needs to carry it now for the rest of his life. I have stood my ground against the bullying and name-calling; there was a high price to pay but my self-respect has been returned to me.

I hope my children are proud of me. I now have the love of a good man. I have the support of some aunts and uncles and friends. Some of them have replaced my parents in my eyes.

You see standing before you here today a frail old man in poor health. No doubt his defence team will make a case that he is an elderly, ill man. But that wasn't an issue when he was raping me so why should it be now?

That said, I am not seeking vengeance here today. I am content with the acknowledgement that I have been wronged, that he did sexually abuse me. I have been vindicated. I am not a liar. I need no longer feel the burning shame or guilt. The damage I have suffered can never be undone but I can walk out of here today and begin a new life knowing that my abuser, my father, has been held responsible for the awful wrong he has done to me.

Self-respect back. Shame and guilt gone. It was never mine to carry. Thank you.

I went back and sat with Jim after delivering my statement. I looked at him. He was crying. We hugged and then held hands, tightly. I still couldn't bring myself to look at my kids. Just then the door opened and in walked Deasún. I smiled at him. Good. He'd been told to stay outside but he'd marched in now and sat down as if to say, 'You won't stop me from supporting my mother.' No one reacted to him being there. He'd be eighteen in a few months, I thought. I'm proud of him. That's my son.

My father's counsel then began going through my father's ailments. A long list. Saying he never left the house. 'What rubbish,' I thought. He was out for meals with his sister, out at Christmas time . . . they went on and on about him needing oxygen as he slept. Rubbish. The judge stopped him and said he'd adjourn proceedings until the following Monday, 21 January, to give him time to go over everything. A week away. I could cope with that.

The judge remanded my father in custody but his counsel stood up and said he wasn't a flight risk. The judge changed his mind and, saying 'Don't take this as a sign of hope', freed him on bail pending his appearance the following Monday. We got up to leave. We stood outside in the hall until my mother and father walked out. They walked past us but neither of them looked at us or said anything.

*

On the way home in the car, in silence, I was thinking over the things that were heard in court. In his statement, according to what Garda Phelan had read out, my father had said he was hard on me because of the way I'd dressed. What bullshit. I was a young child, dressed by my mother, when he first began abusing me. Many times I was in my school uniform. Why wasn't that challenged? I went over everything that was said in that courtroom. Then I snapped out of it. I needed to collect Jack and get home. This was Lewis's last night. He was leaving for America the next day. I had to think of them, think of my family, not my dad, not myself.

We got home quite late, between seven and eight o'clock. I got Jack sorted and into bed. I went back into the sitting room where Jim and the boys were. Lewis's girlfriend was there too. We chatted. My head was pounding. I so needed a bath, time out to sort myself out.

The nine o'clock news came on as we were talking. We weren't paying much attention to it. I was startled when a report came on about my dad. The room went quiet. It showed him and my mother sitting outside the court, having a smoke, as the reporter talked about the charges and about what was said in court. It struck me as funny, really, him puffing away on a cigarette as the reporter described the argument his counsel had made about his poor health. I could see that they were arguing, him and my mother. His face kept twisting in anger. I'd say they were talking about my Victim Impact Statement. I was shocked to see them on the television. It seemed surreal.

*

Six in the morning came quickly. Lewis came in with a cup of coffee for me. I smiled. It was the last time I'd get coffee off him in the morning for a while. I heard him carrying his cases to the car. Tears started welling up but when he came back in to me I didn't let him see them. I didn't ask him to stay, though I wanted to. It was hard enough for him. I got up to see him off. I put my arms around him. I couldn't hide the tears then. I held him close. It hurt, hurt, hurt. He was crying too. 'Go on,' I told him, 'reach for the stars.' His girlfriend was driving him to the airport. I wanted to let them have the last few hours on their own. I stood at the door waving as the car disappeared down the driveway towards the road.

I went into the house and got back into bed. Jim fell asleep but I couldn't so I watched breakfast television. They began talking about the day's newspapers and then they showed the front pages. The *Sun*, the *Star* – 'Ireland's most evil dad'. There was a photo of me and one of my father. Oh my God. The shock. Pure shock. 'Oh my holy God, Jim, Jim, look!' I shouted. I wasn't ready for that. I was so absorbed with whether the case would proceed at all, and then relieved when it did, that it just hadn't occurred to me that it would be all over the papers. My phone began ringing as other people saw it. Lots of calls followed and text messages, good ones, messages of support.

I rang Lewis a little while later. I just wanted to hear his voice. He was at the departure gate at the airport, waiting to board his flight. He sounded sad. 'You can always come home again, you know, son,' I told him. I knew he was scared. Also he hadn't been seeing his girlfriend for very long and yet he had really fallen for her. I just didn't think he knew that himself yet. I was heartbroken for him. 'Don't ask him not to go,' I told myself. 'Just don't, it's not fair.' We finished speaking and I left him to go get his plane.

I turned my phone to silent, closed the curtains and sat in bed, exhausted but unable to sleep. I got more texts from people asking if I was OK. I'd text back 'Yes, I'm fine', but really I didn't know.

Laura decided to remain on for another week, to be in court the following Monday, which was great. I didn't go out much. Jim did the school runs. I just felt so exposed after all the reports about me in the papers, on the television and radio. There were dozens of stories about the case in the papers over the next few days. One stuck out in my mind. It was in the *Star* newspaper and was about my mother standing by my dad. It was reported that my mother said they have nothing to do with me. The newspaper wrote about him living beside a school and a playground. It was the same school my children went to.

One night Laura and I stayed up till all hours talking. I showed her emails from relatives and texts I'd saved. Some of the messages were supportive and backed up my story; others were very harsh and accused me of lying. I played her the secret recording I'd made of my meeting with Richard and Christine when we talked openly about my abuse. I just wanted to make sure Laura believed me, even after my father had pleaded guilty. Laura was finally coming to appreciate the kind of life I'd had and the difficulties I'd faced from the family in trying to get my case to court. I was so glad I'd kept all that stuff, even though, as Laura said, 'You don't have to prove yourself to me.' I guess it was just a habit, something I'd had to do all my life. I was so used to not being believed.

On the Friday night – Laura's last night staying with us – Jim cooked dinner for us and then went off to work. Bless him, he was behind the scenes all that week, keeping things together. I drove up to Bray to drop Laura off the next day, Saturday. It had been so good to have had her come to stay with me, the first time any of my siblings ever did anything like that. We did normal things that sisters do, trying on clothes and the like. I was sad to see her go back to Bray.

I phoned her later that night. She told me she'd gone straight to Christine's and Richard had arrived there. They had had a long chat about everything and she had told them that she believed everything I said and that I had even shown her evidence of it. In the end they agreed they would all go to court on Monday to support me, Christine and her husband and Richard and his partner as well as Laura.

23. My Father Walks Free

Walking towards the court building on Monday 21 January I couldn't help having a feeling of déjà vu. It was Jim and I, Kristel and her boyfriend, Paul, Paddy, Laura, Des and Alice. We had all stayed overnight in the Aisling Hotel. Though we had tried not to talk about what would happen in court over dinner the night before or over breakfast, of course it was playing on everyone's minds.

We got to the steps of the court and all I could see was the flash of camera bulbs going off. We got past them and went in. My stomach began to flutter. That old familiar feeling of nerves had returned.

My dad's brother was there with a few of the same friends and supporters from the week before. A lady approached from the court's victim support service and guided us to the witness suite. We sat there for a while. I was trying to control my nerves. The victim support lady went off somewhere.

We talked about Lewis. I'd spoken to him on the phone the night before. He'd started his new job. I thought he sounded down though. I sensed that he was near to tears on the phone but he was trying to hide it. Oh, how I was missing him. I kept telling him I was OK, that he wasn't to worry about me. I stood up so the others wouldn't see the tears that had come to my eyes as I thought about my son, so far away.

When I looked out the glass windows of the witness suite it looked like people were going into Courtroom Six, where I knew my case would be heard. We all trooped down but when Judge Carney went through his list of cases we learned it wasn't going to be until two o'clock, so we all trooped back to the witness suite again. On the way back we passed the coffee shop and I saw my mother and father sitting there. My father had his bags with him.

It was 11.30 a.m. We had a long wait ahead of us. It seemed like a lifetime. I just wanted it to be done. Over. No more adjournments, no more delays. Finished. I had some soup and chatted to my family. I willed it to be two o'clock. At 1.45 p.m. we returned to the courtroom. I went inside to get my seat. At this stage it felt like that seat had my name on it. I looked around and saw Christine standing at the back of the court. I was surprised she'd come in, I thought she'd have waited outside.

The director of nursing services with the Irish Prison Service was brought into court to speak about the level of care available to someone of my father's age with the health issues he had. Frances Nangle O'Connor told prosecuting counsel that the prison service have managed patients with similar conditions to my father's. She said that the level of care available to him would be as good as that in the general community, and that the oxygen he needed to be on for eight hours a day could be provided.

Mr Justice Carney then asked Monika Leech whether the DPP wanted a prison sentence to be served and if she would stand over any prison sentence he imposed. She said her only instruction was that the DPP viewed the case as falling at the lower level of the upper end of the scale of offences but that the sentence was a matter for the court.

Judge Carney then said he'd made his decision in the last five minutes. 'If I impose a serious custodial sentence and suspend it, it will go out in sound bites, as these things do, that in one of the most serious cases of serial rape of a daughter, the man walked. That is all the community will be told,' he said. 'On the other side if I impose a heavy sentence unsuspended I will be branded as a trial judge who substituted one injustice for another. I am trying to strike a balance.'

Mr Justice Carney then spoke about another judgment, the Kennedy case, in which the Court of Criminal Appeal suspended a moderate sentence imposed on the grounds of the health of the defendant. He said he was 'horrified' in that judgment to find the DPP, 'behind my back, saying it's "a matter of indifference" whether that accused served a prison sentence or not'.

I don't really understand what point the judge is making. The last part of what he's said has gone over my head. Still though, I feel that he's getting close to announcing his decision. I'm conscious of my body stiffening. Anxiety begins to gnaw at me. It feels like everything has slowed down. He is still speaking. I realize, to my horror, that he's praising my dad.

He's talking about his remorse, his good character, his early guilty plea. What remorse? My father has never expressed remorse to me. He mentions my father's history of employment. Then he notes the length of time since the offences. So that makes it all right then? That he hasn't offended since he abused me? Didn't he hear my Victim Impact Statement? I feel my body shake. I'm going to lose control. Oh God. I turn to Jim, bury my head in his shoulder. 'He's going to get away with it,' I whisper to him. 'This has all been for nothing.' Judge Carney continues, saying he is sentencing my father to twelve years with nine of those years suspended. My brain is trying to catch up. What? Twelve years? Nine suspended? So three years?

Three years. He then directs my father's solicitor to apply for bail, pending an appeal. What? What's he saying? What does he mean? Bail? He's walking free? Oh God, he's not going to walk free, is he?

I started to cry. I could feel my shoulders moving. My whole body was racked by sobs. I tried to stop but it only made it worse. I could feel people's arms around me. Jim tried to move me, tried to get me to stand up. I raised my head and became aware that the next case was starting. I couldn't really see through my tears. I was embarrassed to be crying like that in public. Jim took my arm and led me outside. Paddy had his back to me, his hands over his face, sobbing. I went to go towards him but the DPP's counsel, Monika Leech, stopped me. She took me through a door, into a room. She explained what had happened. I didn't want to know. I wanted to go to my kids, to be with them. She had tears in her eyes. So did Garda Phelan. Jim was crying too.

I was still crying myself. There was a glass panel in the door and I kept looking out, at my family gathered outside. I wasn't listening to what Monika Leech was saying at all. I said to her, 'Just let me out to my kids.' She knew I wasn't taking in what she was saying to me so she opened the door and I went out to Paddy and Kristel and Laura. Laura was crying too. I looked around. Everyone was crying. I didn't know which way to turn or who to go to. I hugged my kids, then Laura. Then Richard hugged me. I said to him again that it had all been for nothing.

I was conscious then of my father walking out of the courtroom. We all turned to look at him. He didn't look at us. He walked away in the opposite direction. I just wanted to get out, to flee the court. I started to walk towards the stairs. I'd been told that Christine and Richard had decided they'd walk out of court with me in a gesture of solidarity. I had already asked Jim and Paddy to leave with me, walking shoulder to shoulder, to give me strength, and that's what they did.

I'd prepared a statement as I knew the media would be waiting outside, given the attention the case had got in the press the week before. But it was no good now. I didn't have one for my father walking free from court. It wasn't supposed to be like that. We were surrounded by reporters, television and press cameras. I tried to stop crying, I felt so exposed, them taking pictures of me in tears. I was asked how I was feeling. 'Devastated,' I said. 'Not a day, not a day behind bars.' I can't remember what else I said, I was in shock. I had such a feeling of being exposed, I felt like the cameras could see inside me. I just wanted to get out of there. I wanted to stop them looking inside me.

I walked away with Jim and Paddy. Kristel was walking with Paul, she was crying. He had his arms around her. Paddy had tears running down his face. I stopped to wipe them away. As we began walking back towards the hotel I could hear car horns beeping. My father was walking towards the bus stop. Reporters were running after him. I stood for a minute and watched. Paddy shouted 'Rapist!'

after him. I pleaded with him to stop. 'Let's just go, please, son, I need to get back to the hotel,' I told him.

We walked into the lobby of the hotel. I was conscious of how I must have looked, tears and make-up running down my face. I asked for the key to the room and whether my family could all come up with me. They said it was no problem. I got the feeling they'd heard the news. When we got to the room everyone was quiet. We didn't know what to say to one another. The hotel sent up tea and coffee for everyone. I thought how nice it was of them to do that. We all just sat there for a while, no one saying very much.

Laura and I had agreed to talk to a reporter, Patrick O'Connell, from the *Star*, so after a cup of coffee everyone left and we did the interview together.

Somewhere in the middle of all this going on someone told me Lewis was on his way home. It was hard to take it in. I gathered myself and did the interview. Laura and I had our photo taken together to go with the article. I felt so tired after we finished, just bone weary. We collected our things and went to the car.

When we went to settle our hotel bill they wouldn't take any money from us for the teas and coffees and the girls at reception gave me a card. I was very touched by that. What a kind thing for them to do.

We left for home. It would take almost two hours and we had to collect Jack along the way. We drove home in silence, still not knowing what to say to each other, Jim and I. We dropped Laura at her in-laws in Bray first.

We got home in time to see the nine o'clock news. We watched coverage of the day's events. My phone was going mad with people ringing, a lot of numbers I didn't recognize but others too, relatives, friends and supporters saying how sorry they were at how things had turned out.

I fell into bed that night, exhausted, but I didn't sleep much and was awake at 5.30 a.m. I felt so low. I didn't want to get out of bed. The story was all over the radio news. I knew it'd be in all the newspapers too. Jim took Jack to school and went off by himself for a walk. Deasún had gone to school too. I sat on my own, crying. The story was being replayed over and over on the television news. I felt lost. So, so lost. I'd been defeated. After everything I'd been through, everything I put my family through, my father had gotten away with it.

I heard the front door opening and got up. Lewis was standing in the hall. I could hardly believe it. He gave me a long hug. I didn't want to let him go. I was so happy to see him. He'd decided that with everything that was going on at home he wanted to be here. He'd travelled all night to get home. After talking for a while he went to bed for a bit. My phone kept going but I didn't answer it. I just hadn't the wherewithal to.

In the days that followed the story was featured repeatedly on the news and on many different radio and television programmes, *Morning Ireland* and *Drivetime* on RTÉ Radio, *Prime Time* on RTÉ Television, on the *Vincent Browne Show* on TV3, among others.

There were dozens of newspaper articles about the case. It was a talking point throughout that week. Nothing had prepared me for that, for the amount of coverage it got.

Judge Carney's decision to free my father on bail proved a controversial one. It was a huge story in the media. Legal experts were wheeled out to discuss and comment on it on current affairs and news programmes and it was the talk of the country.

I can't remember when it was exactly that I first heard about the Facebook page 'Justice for Fiona' that was set up. I began hearing that hundreds of people were leaving comments on it in support of me and giving out about Judge Carney's ruling. I looked at the page and was gratified to see that so many people had taken the time to leave comments and say nice things about me. It buoyed me up, gave me strength.

I ventured out of the house on the Tuesday after court. I popped out to the shops with Jim. It was so strange seeing pictures of myself on the front of newspapers. I wanted to run and hide. I was happy with the interview I'd done for the *Star* that evening after the court. Patrick O'Connell had written word for word what I'd said. It made things a little easier; knowing people were hearing my words, my thoughts about it all.

Still though, it was hard to handle all the media attention, all the shows talking about me, calling me brave. I didn't feel brave. I'd begun to receive cards as well as the phone calls and texts of support.

There were many, many calls from reporters and researchers from news and current affairs programmes too, all clamouring for interviews. If you can imagine being caught naked in front of thousands of people, the embarrassment of that, that's how I felt.

I cooked a big dinner that Tuesday evening and invited Kristel and Paul over. I just wanted us all together with Lewis being back. I wanted to make sure too that they were all OK. Laura had returned to England that morning. My eyes were all swollen from crying and I knew I looked pale. To take my mind off things I got busy in the kitchen and cooked our favourite dinner: roast chicken, roast potatoes, vegetables, Yorkshire puddings. I turned off the television. I didn't want Jack to see me on the news or hear my name mentioned.

When Kristel came she told me that her phone had been hopping too with phone calls and requests for interviews. She told me about the Facebook page and how it was going, how people were reacting. She said she'd like to do something to help. I told her I couldn't put my face out there, I didn't feel able to, but that she could go ahead and do what she wanted to, that she had my support. She was worried that she'd cause me grief.

I told them all, as we sat down in the sitting room with the fire lit, all of us eating dinner off our laps because there wasn't room for everyone around the dinner table, that nothing they could say or do would let me down, that they could do what they wanted to help and that they didn't need to run things by me.

After dinner Kristel got on the phone and the next thing I knew there was talk of protest marches being organized in Dublin and Bray and media interviews were being set up.

When Jack went to bed we put on the evening news to see that everyone was still talking about what had happened. It'd been raised on the floor of the Dáil that day. Fianna Fáil

TD Billy Kelleher had raised it but he'd been told by the Ceann Comhairle, Seán Barrett, that the chamber couldn't discuss a decision of the court or criticize those who make such decisions. Deputy Kelleher said he was raising it because of the legitimate concerns of Irish people and the 'huge anger' at the verdict, which had led to calls for a review of sentencing guidelines in Irish courts.

While Deputy Kelleher was stopped by the Ceann Comhairle from saying too much about it, his comments did lead to a response from the Taoiseach, Enda Kenny. He said that my father's case 'had filled the nation with revulsion'. He also said he hoped the case and its outcome so far wouldn't discourage others from coming forward. Little did I know at that time that I would end up meeting him and discussing my case, and concerns around it, within a couple of weeks.

I could feel my mood begin to lift. Later that night I went on Facebook and read through some of the many messages people had left. It was such a help. I held the crystal angel my Aunt Alice had given me tightly in my hand as I read the messages, making a fervent wish that things would come right.

The next morning when Jim dropped Jack off at school one of the parents, a girl I knew, gave him an apple pie to bring home to me. It was such a kind gesture. People at the school had come up to him, wishing me well. Parents of children at the school were beginning to recognize my face from the television. Up until then, from the time we moved to north Wexford, I'd kept a low profile.

Kristel rang me to tell me she was doing an interview with breakfast television on TV3. Thousands of people were now leaving comments on Facebook. I couldn't believe it. I started to think that if strangers could take the time to support me the least I could do was to cop on and do my bit. I started by replying to emails and Facebook comments.

My counsellor rang to say she wanted to see me. I decided to collect Jack from school that afternoon so that I could thank the woman who had given me the apple pie. The smiles and warmth I got from people at the school helped me to put one foot in front of the other.

I went to see my counsellor at the Resource Centre in Gorey afterwards that Wednesday afternoon. We talked about me not hiding my feelings, how it was OK to let people know I'd been hurt. We talked about people's reaction to the story. We talked a lot that day, going over my feelings. I was tired by the time it came to an end. I'd had my phone on silent during the session but I could hear it buzzing away in my bag.

Jim was waiting with Jack and Paddy to collect me after I finished. I told them I'd love a piece of cake, that I needed to do something that felt normal. I felt so worn out. We went to a local coffee shop. It was empty as it was fairly late in the evening. I ordered coffee and cake and we began chatting.

The evening news came on the radio. The headline story was about my case – it was going to go back to court the next day. I felt as if I'd been given an electric shock. I was upset to be hearing such news in that way. Why had no one contacted me? I took out my phone and saw that I had missed calls from the detective. I had just enough battery power to text him and ask him to ring me on Jim's mobile.

He phoned back straight away, sorry that I'd heard it on the news. I understood that it was my own fault for not being available to take his call when he rang. He told me it'd be just him going to court, that they were making an application for the court transcripts of what happened on Monday. 'Phew,' I thought, relieved. 'So you don't need me there?' I asked him. I had made plans to take Jack to a local play centre with his friends as a treat. Darragh said he'd call me back in five minutes, that he had another call coming in. When he did it was to tell me that my father would be in court the next day. 'Well, then I'm going too,' I told him.

I asked him what he was going for. Darragh said he didn't know. 'Well, I'll be there,' I repeated. I hung up and told Jim we had to go, that I needed to get home and prepare a dinner for that evening and the next day as we were going to be back in court the next morning. I had to sort Jack and Deasún out as well. In a panic I upped and left, I didn't even get to eat my cake! I went home to get organized. We couldn't afford to stay in a hotel again.

I didn't know what we were going to court for but I was determined to be there. I learned subsequently that the DPP was going back to court to make an application to have my father's bail revoked.

I was preparing dinner that evening when the news came on. It was all about Kristel and her interview that morning on breakfast television on TV3. I asked Jim to turn it off, I didn't want to watch it while Jack was around so we agreed we'd tape it and watch it later.

After dinner Jim and Paddy went to the cinema and I put Jack to bed. Deasún was in the sitting room. I watched

Kristel's interview on the television in my bedroom. It provoked such a range of emotions in me. I felt proud of her and at the same time upset, watching her struggle to compose herself. I could hear and see the pain she was going through. It really brought home to me how my children had suffered as a result of my abuse. I heard a sob from the sitting room and realized Deasún was watching it too. I rang Kristel to say sorry. Sorry for the pain I'd caused her and my other children. I thought I'd protected them from the worst of it but it was obvious now that I hadn't. Deasún came in to me with a cup of coffee as I spoke on the phone to her. He tried to hide the fact that he'd been crying. There was so much hurt around.

My Uncle Des phoned to say he'd come to court with us the next morning. Paddy intended going too. I was shattered with tiredness. My hair needed to be washed for court. I ran a bath and afterwards took a sleeping tablet, I knew I had to. I just wouldn't be able to face court without sleep and I knew it wouldn't come on its own as I worried about what the next day would bring and agonized about my children. I felt sick as well. I hoped I wasn't getting the vomiting bug.

Thursday 24 January dawned bright and cold. Jim woke me at six with tea and toast. He wanted to make sure I'd eaten something before we left. We got on the road at eight o'clock. Traffic was heavy but we got there about 9.50 a.m. There were loads of reporters outside the Central Criminal Court again. We went straight in and made our way to the coffee shop. It all seemed so familiar by that stage.

My mother and father hadn't arrived yet. I'd been told that they'd ordered a taxi to take them to court and when it arrived at their house in Bray and he went to get into it someone had shouted 'Rapist!' at him. The taxi driver realized who he was and told him to get out of the car. Strangely, when I heard that I felt pity. I didn't tell anyone that though.

Reporters approached me as I sat in the coffee shop. They were full of praise for Kristel and her courage in doing the interview on TV3 the day before.

My mother and father arrived then, they came up in the lift. It was a glass one so I could see them. He had a holdall bag with him.

Garda Phelan arrived and I had a chat with him. Then he told me to go on in. I did, taking up the same seat I'd sat in before. There were about twenty reporters seated to my left. I positioned myself in the seat so that when Judge Carney spoke he could see me. 'He can look me in the eye,' I thought.

I am so nervous. I've been rubbing my hands together, over and over. I look at them now. I've made them red and raw. They're sore. Judge Carney is walking in. I am sick with nerves. We all stand up. I begin to feel dizzy. I am glad to sit down again. Brendan Grehan, counsel for the DPP's office, is speaking. He's saying the judge was wrong to grant my father leave to appeal on Monday because the law had changed in 2010 and the court no longer had that power. Now the judge has begun to speak, saying things that are going over my head. I am trying hard to listen and absorb what he is saying. This is so important.

I hear him say he felt the case was a burden. The shock of him saying that is like a slap in the face to me. Imagine him saying that while I am there, the victim in this case.

Now he's explaining that he wanted the advice of other judges on this case. I feel kind of bad for him now, that I've brought this trouble on him, caused him hassle. Wait! What's he saying now? That he regrets the decision he made on Monday and that he is revoking bail. I keep repeating his words in my head, trying to process what I've just heard. My father is to be sent to jail, immediately. He is to be punished, after all, for what he did to me.

As the judge was talking two barristers stood in front of me, talking and blocking my view. I thought, 'How rude.' So I stood up and asked them to move. I could feel everyone look at me but I didn't care. If Judge Carney was talking about me then I wanted him to see me. He went on to say that he offered Fiona Doyle his regrets. 'I express to Ms Doyle my profound regret for the distress that has been caused to her in this case,' he said. He still didn't look at me. That was it. My father was to be placed in custody. The judge started to move on to the next case.

I stood up and turned to face my father as prison officers came to help him to his feet. He looked shocked. I started to feel sorry for him. As he stood up, holding on to his walking frame, I could hear his barrister apply for bail again.

The judge refused and my father started to walk towards the door, not the exit door but the one for prisoners. I kept looking over, thinking he might look at me, but he didn't. I could feel my chest getting tight.

I nearly shouted, 'Stop! Take your hands off him. Don't lock him up.' My mother just sat there. She never moved. Just stared ahead. The door closed. My dad was gone. I felt dejected. 'That's the last I'll see of him,' I thought. I looked at my mother again. Nothing. No reaction. She just sat there, dispassionately. My father's barrister asked her to go outside. I heard Jim say, 'Come on, Fiona, let's go.' I said, 'No, I'm not walking out before my mother.' She stood up and walked out. I went out after her.

Garda Phelan called me so he and I and Monika Leech could speak. Once again my attention wasn't on what they were saying. My mother was sitting on a bench outside the courtroom door. I kept looking at her, wondering how she was feeling. Then I wondered how she would get home. For a minute or two I actually worried about it. I nearly offered her a lift.

I gave my attention to the detective. When I turned back to look at her again a couple of minutes later she was gone. Myself, Jim, Paddy and my Uncle Des headed down the stairs. I could see the reporters gathering outside. I braced myself to face them even though my thoughts were still in complete turmoil. I put a smile on my face. After all, this was the end, wasn't it? This was what I had wanted. I walked out. The cold air hit me in the face. I smiled with relief. I was beginning to take it in. Justice had been done.

Reporters gathered around me. I was aware of television cameras. I was asked again how I felt. I smiled. 'Better than I did on Monday, can't you see it in my face? Justice has been done,' I told them.

I was thinking to myself, 'Maybe now my father will get a taste of how I felt, lonely, isolated, no support, his home comforts gone.' I felt strongly that it was the last time I'd see him. I believed he would probably die in prison. I felt sad again. I walked out of that court an orphan, I felt. No mother or father. I kept looking around to see if there was any sign of my mother. She was nowhere to be seen.

We walked away, went to a coffee shop a few yards away from the courthouse. I sat down with a cup of tea. It all felt very surreal. My phone started going, people ringing to say that they'd heard, that they were happy for me. Asking me if I was celebrating. No, I wasn't. I just wanted to collect my son and go home. I never wanted to have to be there again. Mind you, that could still happen. My father could still appeal. I had asked that he not appeal, as an indication of his remorse. Surely to God he wouldn't?

We drove home to collect Jack. It was really quiet again in the car. 'It's all over,' I kept telling myself, again and again. Thank God for the love and support of so many people who had wrapped me up in their kindness and goodness that week like a warm blanket. The depth of feeling had been so strong. It had kept me going.

I was due to meet with the Taoiseach the next week to discuss my case and issues arising from it. But right then all I wanted was a hug from my innocent five-year-old. A child who didn't even know his maternal grandparents.

24. Explaining Myself to the World

I was asked to appear on *The Late Late Show* the day my father went to jail. I was at home when I got the call about it. My feelings were still all over the place. Everything was so very raw.

I agreed to do it. By now I had had a crash course in the power of the media. As Ireland's number-one talk show *The Late Late Show* would be a good opportunity to say my piece about the system and what was wrong with it. I wanted to talk about changes I'd like to see in the legal system to do with how victims are treated, about minimum sentencing and most importantly about the effects of abuse on individuals, the kinds of feelings they have to live with and how it leads to them going down self-destructive paths.

It was agreed that my interview would be pre-recorded because of the sensitive and adult nature of the topic and for legal reasons. The people working on the show were very good to me and very sensitive to my feelings. Ellen Lynch, who is the ghostwriter of this book, said she would come with me so I would feel comfortable. If there was anything I struggled with she would step in and help.

The experience was quite surreal. Here I was, little old Fiona, going to appear on the biggest talk show in Ireland. It was a show I often watched at home on Friday nights from the comfort of my couch, as do so many hundreds of thousands of others.

Knowing my interview was being pre-recorded helped with my nerves. Before we went to record, Ryan Tubridy came into the room where we were waiting to have a chat, to put me at ease, and he did. He's a really nice guy. He's funny and he made me smile. I'd spoken at length with the show's researcher beforehand so I knew what kind of questions I would be asked and I also knew that if I stuck to the truth I would be fine, and I was. I told my story and I was OK until Ryan asked about my mam and dad. I could feel the tears well up and I tried hard not to cry.

Ryan asked me if I loved them and I answered truthfully, that yes, I did. They are the only parents I have, I said. I told him about nearly having asked my mother if she was OK for a lift home the day my father was jailed.

We could have stayed overnight in Dublin after the show but Ellen and I headed home. I'd promised Jim and my kids that I would come home to watch the show with them. My Uncle Des and Aunt Alice and their daughter Aleesha called to the house to watch it with us. I remember there being a scramble for biscuits to go with our tea as we waited for it to start.

I was nervous. I hadn't told anyone what I'd said in the interview. Would they be angry at me? Everyone was quiet as we sat and watched it. They were quiet for a minute or two when it was finished as well. I think they were all shocked at how open I was, but no one was annoyed or upset with me. They all understood.

I heaved a huge sigh of relief. It had been a long day and

I was exhausted and went to bed after my uncle, aunt and cousin had gone home. Jim and I talked about what I'd said in the interview. As always, he was supportive and loving.

There was a huge and very positive reaction in the days that followed. No one said anything bad or had a go at me but I knew people were probably thinking: 'How could you still have feelings for your parents after what they did to you?' The answer to that is: I said it because it was true. I want to be honest and I want to be me. Not bitter and twisted. Otherwise it would just eat me up, make me old before my time.

Mary Flaherty, the CEO of Children At Risk in Ireland (CARI), the Irish voluntary organization that provides specialized therapy and support to children, families and groups affected by child sexual abuse, had said of Judge Carney's initial decision to grant bail: 'It seems as if the judge has decided to make this a test case . . . While there may be valid legal issues to be highlighted quite appropriately by the judge, and indeed victims' groups are all too aware of the success of perpetrators in using the appeal system to undermine some of the few convictions that succeed in rape and sexual abuse crimes in our State, the re-victimization of Fiona Doyle by Monday's sentencing decision was too high a price to pay.'

She went on to say that it was seriously damaging to public confidence in the legal system that I became a victim in the ongoing dispute between Judge Carney and the Court of Criminal Appeal. 'Thankfully, this has now been acknowledged by the judge. His particular apology to Fiona Doyle for losing sight of her rights in all of this must be some recompense for the failures to date,' she concluded.

Ellen O'Malley-Dunlop, the CEO of the Rape Crisis Centre, also spoke out about my father having been released on bail. 'For her, the amount of time served by her father mattered. The twelve-year sentence handed down by Justice Paul Carney indicated the seriousness of the crimes committed against her as a child; however, having nine years suspended was very upsetting for Fiona Doyle and not an encouraging message for others who had had similar experiences.'

It was great if my painful experiences were serving some good in raising awareness about victims' rights and the sentencing policy. However, it was quite a surprise to find myself in the position to make the case directly to the most important politician in the country within a week of my father going to jail.

The meeting with the Taoiseach, Enda Kenny, came about quite by accident. It was all over the news that he had spoken about my case in the Dáil. The *Star*'s Patrick O'Connell rang me for my reaction and I said I'd heard what the Taoiseach said, but that if he was serious about it he should speak to me directly.

I said that because I was annoyed that Judge Carney hadn't looked me in the face when he'd made his apology. It just felt that he was doing something he felt obliged to do. The reporter did an article on what I said about meeting the Taoiseach, which appeared in the paper the next day. Later the following day I received word from an official at the

Taoiseach's office that he had agreed to meet me. I was pleased. I knew exactly what I wanted to say to him. The meeting was arranged for Wednesday 30 January in the Dáil. A few days later I got a call from the same official to say the Taoiseach had to change the date to the day after as he would be attending the state funeral on the Wednesday of Garda Adrian Donohoe, who had been shot dead during an armed raid. The meeting was fixed for 5.15 p.m. on the Thursday instead. I was told my husband and kids could come with me. I was really pleased about that. My next thought was: 'I need a new dress!'

During those days people were very good to me. I was still getting good wishes, cards and gifts. The owner of a hair salon in Gorey offered to do my hair for me and another lovely lady asked me to let her make my jewellery for the meeting with the Taoiseach. Someone had also gone into a travel agency in Dublin and left payment for a holiday for me and my family. That generous and kind man wished to remain anonymous. I was deeply touched by his gesture and we did avail ourselves of the holiday later, using it to take a badly needed break after all that had gone on.

I was excited at the prospect of meeting someone in such high office in the government. On the day I woke early and was up at 5.30 a.m. I had my hair done at the salon in Gorey where Kay and the girls were so nice to me. We left for Dublin afterwards.

We were met by an official when we got to the Dáil and taken to a boardroom. We waited for about ten minutes and then the Taoiseach walked in. He had only one member of his staff with him, his private secretary, I think. He kissed me and introduced himself, then turned and shook hands with Jim and Kristel and the boys. He joked with Kristel and the boys.

He sat down beside me and started to ask me questions. He turned to Jim and asked him when he'd first been told about my past. Jim told him we'd discussed it before we got married.

He told him about us going away to Barbados to get married on our own, how upset I was that my kids weren't there and how that was done because I didn't want my parents to be present. Jim was getting upset as he spoke. I could see that the Taoiseach was moved by what he was saying.

He asked me about my mother. I told him about the constant name-calling I'd endured. I told him I couldn't say what those names were because I didn't want to swear in front of him but he told me it was OK, so I told him some of the names I was called.

I told him about the places where my father would rape me. He asked me about teachers at schools I'd attended and hospitals I'd been taken to for treatment, if anything was done. I told him about buying a video camera to record that meeting I'd had with my brother and sister, how desperate I'd been to prove I wasn't lying about the abuse. I asked him if he could arrange a meeting for me with the Garda Commissioner, explaining that I needed answers regarding my first complaint.

He spoke about me being brave in forgoing my anonymity to speak out about my case. I responded by asking him, if he was trying to bring in legislation, trying to get it through the Dáil, something he felt passionate about, really passionate, and a lot of people were depending on it, but to get it passed he would have to stand naked in the middle of Dublin, would he do it? Well, I could see from the expression on his face that he was very taken aback to be asked that. He didn't give me an answer.

I felt kind of bad then, putting him on the spot like that, but I told him that was how I felt, naked and exposed, but that I felt I had to do it to see my father named and shamed for what he'd done. I'd done so in the hope of helping other abuse victims.

He spoke to Kristel about when I'd first told her about my past, and he asked Paddy and Lewis the same. We went on to talk about the courts system and about the garda who investigated my case. I couldn't praise Darragh Phelan highly enough, I told him, but it was a different story with the courts. I described how I felt as though my feelings weren't considered. I was trying to get across to him how badly I was made to feel by the system. Like, for example, how some family weren't allowed into court. Some small changes would really help, I said.

I went on to tell him how worthless the light sentence had made me feel, as if I somehow wasn't worth more than the few short years that were imposed. That said, I told him I was aware of my own conflicting feelings, that I'd thought, before sentencing, that proving I wasn't a liar would be enough, but it turned out not to be. I needed to feel that my life was important, that it had some worth, and that what happened to me should be acknowledged as grossly wrong and punished accordingly.

We talked about my suicide attempts. As we spoke I was

conscious of the atmosphere in the room – heavy and sad – so I tried to lighten it up by joking with the Taoiseach too. He asked me about my future, I told him I wasn't thinking too far ahead, that my first priority was to finish this book so that my story, my whole story, would be put on record.

The interview ended soon afterwards. I thanked the Taoiseach for his time. I felt it had been a good meeting, constructive, and that he had been genuine in listening to me and taking on board what we'd discussed. I said as much to the media who were waiting outside as we left Leinster House that evening.

25. Letters to My Family

I have found, over the years, that writing down my thoughts and feelings has been a release for me. When I couldn't talk to anyone about my abuse, I committed my thoughts to paper. At least, I thought, I'd have a record for myself, if no one else. There was one stage in my life though, which I've mentioned, when I felt unable to do that. I put what I'd written away and didn't start writing again for nearly four years. When I did so it was prompted by the realization that Kristel, at fourteen, was growing up and that one day, when she was older, I'd like her to know about my past, in order for her to better understand me. I didn't think I'd be able to sit her down and tell her to her face though, so I thought that keeping a record of it and showing it to her would be best. I thought I'd deal with the boys in the same way, when they too were older.

Now that I'm almost at the end of my story I'm turning once again to writing to put my thoughts and feelings into some kind of order. The letters that follow, to my daughter Kelly, my daughter Kristel, and my sons, to Jim, to my brothers and sisters, my father, uncles, aunts and cousins, are an attempt to lay out how I see things at this point in my life. It's the best way I have of doing so.

Dear Kelly,

Kelly, nothing will ever change the fact that I am your mam. You are my first-born child and I love you and always will. I know you don't want to hear that, but as a mother yourself now you should understand it. Imagine someone telling you not to love your child. It doesn't and won't work.

I am not going to criticize my parents to you as it's quite clear you love them. I will respect that. But you also have wonderful brothers and a sister. They never did anything to you. They would be fantastic aunt and uncles to your kids.

I had hoped that through the court cases you would finally learn the truth but you didn't come into court, you just sat outside. I think you have a big fear of the truth, which I understand. Maybe someday you will be ready for it.

I know you are not happy with me speaking out, but I needed to have my voice heard. It wasn't done to hurt you or your children. I would never do that. I have never set out to hurt anyone, even Mam and Dad. I needed justice. I needed to stand up for myself and not fear the truth coming out.

I really wish things had been different, for me and for all of you, but it was the cards we were dealt. The truth, as hard and as awful as it is, should not pull us apart. I hope you won't let it destroy us. I only want the very best for you and your children, and if you feel it's best they don't know about me then I will respect that, and I will respect you and your support of my father and mother.

It's important to me that you know that if you ever change your mind I will be here and my door will be open, as will my heart. I hope your children will someday realize they have a nanny out there that loves them and would love to be part of their lives. As it should be. For you, Kelly, I wish happiness and love, and the very best life with your husband.

Your mam, always.

Fiona

Dad,

I find it hard calling you 'Dad', because you never were. How could you have been? Rape, abuse – physical and mental – was all I knew. You controlled me. You taught me things no child should know. But, worst of all, you didn't see any wrong in it. You would blackmail me with threats of suicide and, as I got older, you became possessive, like a jealous boyfriend.

When I finally got the sex abuse to stop the mental abuse got worse, you constantly put me down, called me a liar. It never stopped. You helped in the cover-up about Austin because deep down you knew; you knew where he got it from. You helped in poisoning my daughter against me.

But there was one thing you never reckoned on. That was me. Me, Dad, weak Fiona turned into a strong adult. One that would do anything to protect her kids and grandchildren. You never for a second believed I had the strength to do it, and when I went to the gardaí a second time you weren't too worried, were you? You just kept up the united front with Mam, both protecting yourselves, trying to make little of me. Even in your statements you tried to belittle me, talking about my clothes, how I dressed. Did you forget I was a young child when you started abusing me? How could you have talked so casually about digitally penetrating me?

I worried about you going to prison but now that you are

there I don't worry any more. In fact I hardly think of you, because I know you are not sorry, you have no remorse. Sure, how could you have when you still see no wrong in what you did? You are still lying even, still telling some of your family you didn't do it. Are you lonely, Dad? Do you feel out of control of your life? Are you getting counselling? Do you miss your home comforts?

Dad, I don't hate you but I do hope one day you realize what you did to me. You said it to me once before, that you knew that you ruined my life, so on some level you seem to have some realization of the harm you did me. But then you denied having said that. I didn't take you to court because of hate, I did it for justice, and I got it, finally. You do deserve to be where you are. You and I are finished now, Dad, we will never speak again, or probably set eyes on each other. I hope you get help in there. I, meanwhile, will get on with my life with no shame or guilt any more. That is yours now to carry.

I feel sorry for you.
Fiona

Dear Austin,

Oh boy, my big brother, I miss you. I wonder, what would you think of everything: Mam and Dad, the court cases?

You killed yourself and we miss you, we all do. You did awful things, really unforgivable stuff. In my eyes you said sorry when you took your own life. But, sure, what else could you have learned? There was no teaching right and wrong in our house, no guidance, no good role models for us to follow. We were on our own. All I had was you. I look back at the

*hard childhood you had. You went through hell. I used to feel
so sorry for you. Constant beatings. I remember Dad upturn-
ing the bed with you in it. I went to your funeral to say goodbye
and to tell you I loved you. I am so sad you are gone but I
can't put up a photo of you in my house even now, I am still
struggling with what you did.*

*I do believe that you watched over me through everything, I
really do, and I do talk to you a lot, as you know. We are all so
broken. Watch over us all, Austin, please. I tried to put right a
big wrong and I don't think I will rest until it is fully put right.
We will never be fixed, Austin. We will see each other again.
Until then I will miss you.*

All my love, my big brother,
Fiona

Dear Christine,

*I am in a lot of pain over what has happened between us and
I'm sad that you were not in a position to be by my side during
the court case. You were upset with me for telling your children
about my past but, Christine, they were adults and I couldn't lie
any more.*

*There was deep damage done to me for many years. I was not,
and am not, the source of the problems in our family. It took me
years to understand that myself. I'm not sure you understand
that. It's very hard for me to cope with that. I hope that someday
you will see me and the past in a different light.*

*Until then, I have chosen to walk away from you. That was
hard to do. It hurts. I will always miss you. I will always love
you. I won't ever hurt you.*

I wish you well, sis, but I'm sad to say I can't be a part of

*your life. I hope someday you will get the counselling I think
would help you.*

    Be happy and well.

   All my love,

    Fiona

My dearest sister Laura,

   *You, my sister, have been the light at the end of my tunnel.
You realized that Dad was guilty and when you did you said
sorry. Sorry for not believing me before that. Sis, it meant the
world to me. I'm crying as I write this.*

   *When we talk about our childhood you remember how I
minded you, dressed you when you had accidents (and you had a
few!), looked out for you.*

   *I have so much hope for us. Your support at the time of the
court cases was amazing. Coming to stay with me at my house
that week, I loved having you here. I'd never had any of you
stay before. It meant so much. I felt so welcome when I went to
stay with you last summer. Your kids are amazing, they remind
me so much of my own.*

   *I think finally we will have the bond sisters should have and
things will only get better for us.*

   *I hope nothing will ever come between us again. I have my
nieces and nephew back. My kids have cousins back. I will
always be here for you, my lovely sister. I love you and need you.*

   All my love,

    Your big sis Fiona

Dear Richard,

   You are the little brother I loved so much and would worry about. We fought and didn't see eye to eye, but all I ever wanted to do was mind and protect you.

I know you did try to support me, but you were torn. I could see that. That hurt. Many's the time I left your home in tears.

I never intended doing anything to hurt you. I wish you could see that and realize it's true.

I would love that the entire family would join me in counselling so that we would come to realize the damage our parents did to us. Though I was the one who was sexually abused, we all bear emotional scars.

I need to mind me now. You may not agree with my memories and my account of what I suffered, but everyone's views will be different due to the age difference between us.

I truly wish you the very best, and hope that someday things can be different.

All my love,

Your big sister Fiona

To my wonderful children, Kristel, Patrick, Lewis, Deasún and Jack,

You are all the lights in my life. You are my life. I am so proud of you all. The love and support I have received from you all has had no bounds, when we talked in October 2011 about me going to the gardaí I worried about the effects it would have on your lives. I needn't have worried though, because you didn't care, you were behind me 100 per cent. You never had any thoughts about yourselves, only me. I was so touched by that.

I had to show you what I wrote about my life. No mother should have to tell her kids such awful stuff. I could see the hurt on your faces. I felt so bad. You all knew I wasn't responsible for it though. All you ever wanted was the truth to come out for my sake and I wanted to do it for your sake so you would never have to be in a position where you would have to defend me. And we did it, all of us together. What great kids you are.

Kristel, you are doing so well, you have your own home, you have a great boyfriend with a wonderful family. I am so proud of you. As for my boys, all you big lads, I feel so protected with you all around me. I will always love, cherish, protect and push and support you.

My kids, I want you to reach for the stars, to push yourselves for better, to be better, never just settle for second best. Treat people as you like to be treated and you will never go wrong. Cherish your partners, respect them and never raise your hands to anyone. I know you all will always make me proud. I trust you all with my life, none of you could ever do me wrong, which is as it should be. Your home will always be with me. Be strong and always stand up for the truth.

Your proud, proud and loving mother
Xxxxx

My dearest Jim,

You, my love, are the most amazing man. You stood by me through thick and thin. You never once asked me not to do this. In fact, in times when I would be in tears with no strength to go on you would push me. You carried me, gave me strength. You took care of the house, our kids; you did it all, when there were days I couldn't get out of bed. You never complained. You did the school runs, the shopping, cleaning, making dinners.

At the court cases you were my protector standing with me. On some occasions you held me up. You and I have been through so much together. We faced your demon — you gave up alcohol for me and you never once faltered and went back to it. You and I, Jim, have such a deep, deep love, a love that previously I had only ever known for my kids. I am the luckiest woman to have found you. I would give my life for you, my hubby. We do everything together and never get tired of each other.

I thank you, my love, for everything. For our son, Jack. For the Doyle name. I hope I can make your family proud of me as I am of them. I love your mum. Finally I am a part of a good family. You are a wonderful dad to all my kids and they love and respect you so much. You are the dad they never had.

Jim, you told me to go do what I need to do and I will. I feel now I need to speak out, to talk about the effects of rape and abuse. I want and feel a need to help people that have gone through abuse, and help pave the way for them to feel comfortable going to the authorities. Anything I can do, you, you wonderful man, said you will support me in. How kind and loving that is. That's the love we have and I have no doubt it will go on for ever.

Thank you, my hubby, thank you.

You wife and best friend for ever,

Fiona

To my uncles, aunts and cousins,

When I was growing up I would look at you all and wonder: what happened to mine? My mam and dad? How was it that you were all so nice and kind? The nights I spent in your homes that I'd close my eyes and pray that when I woke up you would be my mam and dad, my brothers and sisters. It made me realize how bad things were in our house. We would be made to stay away from your houses for months on end due to a row or something and I would miss you so much. I'd sneak off to see you. As I grew into an adult I wanted to be with you all more, you were all such kind, loveable, supportive people and I felt strongly that my kids would benefit from being around you so I told you all the truth about my life.

Some of you couldn't handle it, some of you put some distance between us and I know it was due to my own actions. Some of you stood up to support me and most of all my kids.

Des and Alice especially, you became my family. With your support and advice you picked up the pieces so many times. Jess, Mac, Aleesha, you were there to give me breaks and to babysit for me. I have such a bond with you guys; you mean the world to me.

Some of you struggled with the truth, just couldn't handle it. I tried to understand your doubt but it upset me and, at times, made me angry. I'm not angry now. I just need time to heal and then I'd like to meet with you and maybe we can talk about it.

To those of you who still don't believe my father abused me, well, guess what? I don't care any more. If you cannot see and accept the truth then I'm not going to worry about it.

I've gotten to know cousins again and see what great people you are. I love having you all in my life. The person I am today was partly your doing, my kids being the adults they are was also your doing, so I can't thank you enough, except to say be proud, proud of the decent people you are. You will always have a special place in my heart and in the hearts of my children.

I love you all so much.
Your niece and cousin,
Fiona (Yo Yo)

Mother . . .

No, I'm not going to do it. There's nothing I want to say in a letter to my mother that I would want to put in this book.

Epilogue

Here I am, forty-seven this year and life has been so hard and yet so rewarding. It sounds strange to say that, I know. I'm not going to go back over my childhood; I've just laid all that out in this book. What I mean is: how many people get to have their dreams come true? I dreamed about getting justice and being vindicated. I dreamed about being listened to. I dreamed about writing this book. I dreamed about making a difference. I dreamed about finding true love and raising good children. Those things have finally happened for me.

I believe in positive thinking and that anything is possible. I now have life on the 'other side'. The other side of guilt and shame. Other abuse and rape victims who have experienced justice will know what I mean. My wish would be that every abuse victim would get a chance at life without that shame and guilt. It does not belong to them but to the perpetrators of their abuse.

It's such an awful subject and I've always had a strong feeling of not wanting to taint other people with the details of my abuse. I found writing about my First Communion both shocking and upsetting. The reason I could write about it in such detail in this book is because I'd already written about it for my Victim Impact Statement.

I remember the night I did so. It was the end of November 2012. Darragh Phelan had advised me, in writing my statement, to include a specific incident of abuse which had particular significance so that it would make a greater impact. My First Communion, for example. I sat up all night, making myself remember what had happened forty years earlier. I couldn't believe what I recalled, the details and my feelings, when I concentrated on what I'd tried to bury for four decades. An image of me lying there that night played in my mind. It was as if I were watching a video. I was standing up, looking down at a little girl. I could hardly see her with the body on top of her, just her head sticking out from under him as he held on to the arm of the sofa to help him with thrusting into her. I looked at the face, my face, and saw no expression. Only a pair of big brown eyes looking up. People would say I had lovely brown eyes, but as I looked at them I saw how sad that little girl was. I saw tears and pain. I was crying as I remembered and wrote that November night last year, making myself go back to that place, to those feelings. I just want to cuddle that little girl, put my arms around her and protect her.

Boy it was so difficult, how did I get through it day after day, rape after rape? Then I wondered, how will I cope with the feelings writing this has brought up? After I'd finished writing it and read it over in November I decided I could not read it out in court. It was too graphic, too shocking. I couldn't do it. I couldn't have people listen to it. Adults listen to it. Yet, as a seven-year-old, I had had to handle the reality of it day after day.

I headed in to my counsellor the next day and read it to her and cried again. I felt sick to the pit of my stomach. I was angry, too, as I have so often been, when memories of my abuse come flooding back.

So I wanted to include the details in this book, hard as it is to read them. I didn't want to sugar-coat it. The reality is that abuse is awful. Awful. Awful.

One other shocking thing going back over that memory brought up for me was the realization that, although as an adult I wash every day – daily showering is the done thing – as a child I didn't. We only had a bath once a week in our house. So it raises something else for me and that is how I must have been going around smelling bad because I was having sexual intercourse and not washing. As a child, I must have given off horrible smells that would have been unfamiliar to other children. No wonder I had no friends. Is this why I was so alone in school? And is it the reason my mother had such an issue with the knickers in the wash, the beatings as a little girl if I forgot to change my pants or if I put them in the laundry basket without rinsing them out myself first? She would call me names if I forgot. 'You dirty, smelly bitch!' and I'd get a slap in the face and she would tell my dad, 'That one is a dirty bitch, she doesn't even change her knickers.'

Going public for me has been the best decision ever. I can meet people now and not have to explain myself. They know. They understand. They support me. That support, the blanket of love and warmth that people wrapped around me – well, nobody has any idea how much that helped me and gave me strength in those dark days.

When I think back now over the things that have happened since the first court date, I can scarcely believe all that's gone on.

First, that contentious judgment of Mr Justice Paul Carney. I knew nothing about Judge Carney before 14 January. I didn't know that he had caused controversy with previous rulings. I didn't know that sentences he handed down were often, to his chagrin, overturned in the Court of Criminal Appeal on the grounds of being either too lenient or too harsh. I didn't know of his frustration as a result of what he saw as their inconsistent application of sentencing guidelines. I wasn't aware that he'd spoken publicly about how constrained he'd felt in passing sentencing in rape and sexual assault cases as a result or how it had come to affect his sentencing decisions. I certainly had no way of knowing that he'd choose 'my' case, imposing a largely suspended sentence and then freeing my father on bail, to highlight the issue. In doing so he caused me and my family much added grief and upset.

When I came to learn the background to the judge's ruling that day, I thought that it had backfired on him. He came in for much criticism over it. On reflection though, I believe his actions had the desired effect, bringing attention to the rulings of the Court of Criminal Appeal.

Shortly after my father went to jail the office of the DPP announced that it was to appeal the lightness of the sentence. When she heard that, Eileen O'Malley-Dunlop welcomed the decision, saying it was 'a very positive decision for other victims. It will also have far-reaching positive effects for the safety of Irish society. It sends a message to perpetrators of these crimes that they will be punished appropriately.'

I'd wondered many times, as I fought to get my case against my father into court, whatever happened to the first garda complaint I'd made. After Judge Carney's change of heart and my father's bail being revoked, I travelled up to Bray one day. I wanted to meet people from the Oldcourt estate, former neighbours of mine and still neighbours of my mother. I wanted them to know that I had no bad feelings towards anyone in the estate, which had been repeatedly mentioned in the media coverage that followed the case. The majority of people in Oldcourt are good, decent people. Most of them would have been unaware of my abuse. Indeed for most of them, viewing our family, they'd have seen a daughter who was on good terms and had a lot of interaction with her parents and siblings, as I was, for much of those years, keeping in with them so that I could see Kelly and be involved in her life. I went along to the Resource Centre in Oldcourt that day and spoke with a number of residents. They were warm and supportive.

Afterwards, as I prepared to leave, I got a phone call from Bray Garda Station. A sergeant there told me she'd been directed to find the file on my first complaint. I wasn't told who gave this order or why. I had mentioned publicly that I intended seeking a meeting with the Garda Commissioner about the missing file so I guessed it was to do with that.

At the station the garda asked me where she might start looking for the file. I suggested that my HSE files might contain information on it, and also to contact the council as the social worker had told them about my situation in order to get me moved. She should speak to my family too, I said. My sister Laura remembered the gardaí coming to my parents' house on foot of my complaint; she was living there at the time.

I left the garda station in Bray that day with renewed hope that the file would be found and I would perhaps get a proper answer to why that first complaint wasn't pursued. It wasn't to be though. The sergeant rang me in early April to say she had been unable to find any record of it. I was shocked. I asked her if she'd read the HSE files and she said she had. I asked her if she'd spoken with my former social worker and she said she hadn't. I asked why not and she told me it was because it was an internal investigation.

It was some weeks later when I was going through my own files, the few that had been released to me from the HSE in response to a Freedom of Information request, that I came across a letter from the social worker about my annulment, in which she clearly stated that she supported me in making my statement to the gardaí. There it was – further proof that I had made a complaint previously.

It is my intention not to let the matter lie. It is too serious for that. If abuse victims are to have confidence in the justice system then they need to know that when they do make a complaint, it will be followed up properly.

One of the most satisfying things for me about my father being prosecuted, finally, was that I got to speak out. After being silent for so many years, I found my voice and it was finally heard. Though it was strange to be catapulted into the media spotlight, and I felt uncomfortable at first, it began to dawn on me how the power of the media can be used to get a message across and bring about positive change.

Having appeared on *The Late Late Show* and met the Taoiseach, I also got to meet President Michael D. Higgins at Áras an Uachtaráin at a reception to mark International Women's Day. At that reception many important and influential women from various agencies and sectors across Ireland came up to me and congratulated me on speaking out. Their endorsement was so gratifying. I met with Ellen O'Malley-Dunlop for the first time. I've since undertaken some work in support of the Dublin Rape Crisis Centre.

I am not full of hate and anger. I don't want to be like that. I am not a man-hater. Boys are just as much at risk of being abused, and men too get abused. Men have approached me since my case, wishing me luck.

What I really want to do is speak. Having found my voice, I want to continue to speak out. Speaking out is power, and people seem willing to listen so I will speak out as much as I can. I can talk about my experience; tell people about my battle; and, yes, it was a battle. Hearing it will make it easier for the next person, I hope.

So I thank you all. I thank you for buying this book and reading my story. I hope it's given you a deeper understanding of the effects of rape and abuse.

I hope, for anyone that has suffered abuse and hasn't come forward, that it will give you the strength to do so. I hope that all victims of rape and abuse can go on to live life without shame and guilt.

All my thanks,

Fiona

Acknowledgements

I cannot thank enough Garda Darragh Phelan, who investigated the case against my father and got it to court, for his dedication, diligence and patience throughout.

Thanks and deep gratitude to Ellen Lynch, the ghostwriter of this book, who believed from the start my story was worth telling and worked countless hours over a year and a half to put shape and structure on it.

Thanks to everyone at Penguin for their faith in the book and seeing it through to publication.

Thanks to my husband, Jim, who never once asked me to stop, and who held us all together; to my daughter Kristel, and sons Paddy, Lewis, Deasún and Jack for their love and support throughout; and to my uncle and aunt, Des and Alice Burke, and their children, Alan, Jessica, Aleesha and Mac – you picked up me and my children so many times.

Finally, to the people of Ireland and beyond I thank you for your love and the blanket of support you wrapped around me.

He just wanted a decent book to read ...

Not too much to ask, is it? It was in 1935 when Allen Lane, Managing Director of Bodley Head Publishers, stood on a platform at Exeter railway station looking for something good to read on his journey back to London. His choice was limited to popular magazines and poor-quality paperbacks – the same choice faced every day by the vast majority of readers, few of whom could afford hardbacks. Lane's disappointment and subsequent anger at the range of books generally available led him to found a company – and change the world.

'We believed in the existence in this country of a vast reading public for intelligent books at a low price, and staked everything on it'
Sir Allen Lane, 1902–1970, founder of Penguin Books

The quality paperback had arrived – and not just in bookshops. Lane was adamant that his Penguins should appear in chain stores and tobacconists, and should cost no more than a packet of cigarettes.

Reading habits (and cigarette prices) have changed since 1935, but Penguin still believes in publishing the best books for everybody to enjoy. We still believe that good design costs no more than bad design, and we still believe that quality books published passionately and responsibly make the world a better place.

So wherever you see the little bird – whether it's on a piece of prize-winning literary fiction or a celebrity autobiography, political tour de force or historical masterpiece, a serial-killer thriller, reference book, world classic or a piece of pure escapism – you can bet that it represents the very best that the genre has to offer.

Whatever you like to read – trust Penguin.

Fiona Doyle was born in south Dublin in 1965. She now lives in
~~~~~~~~~~~~~~~~~~~~~~~~ ...y. She has received People of the
Year, *Irish Tatler* Woman of the Year and Pride of Ireland awards for
her bravery in coming forward to tell her story.